EARTHSONG

A Green Anthology of
Poetry, Readings and Prayers

EARTHSONG

A Green Anthology of Poetry, Readings and Prayers

COMPILED BY

ERNA and MICHAEL COLEBROOK

CHURCHMAN PUBLISHING
1990

Earthsong
A Green Anthology of Poetry, Readings and Prayers
compiled by
Erna and Michael Colebrook
was first published in 1990 by
Churchman Publishing Limited
117 Broomfield Avenue
Worthing, West Sussex BN14 7SF

Publisher: Peter Smith

Agents in
Dublin; Sydney; Wellington;
Kingston, Ontario and Wilton, Connecticut

Distributed to the Book Trade by
Bailey Book Distribution Limited
(a division of the Bailey and Swinfen Holdings Group)
Warner House, Wear Bay Road
Folkestone, Kent CT19 6PH

Represented to the Home Book Trade by
Christian Publishers' Representatives
Holy Trinity Church
Marylebone Road
London NW1 4DU

ISBN 1 85093 187 9

Printed in Great Britain
on recycled paper by
Bourne Press Limited of Bournemouth

For our children, Peter and Julia,
and in memory of Helen.

Contents

No water can vanish my fire
No fire can melt my metal
No metal can cast my mould
No mould can capture my image
No image can reflect my aura

For

I am the deep of the ocean
I am the flash of the darkness
I am the smile of the tear
I am the peak of the depth
I am eternity of the moment
I am the poet

Shruti Pankaj.

Acknowledgements

It could be argued that compiling this anthology was like writing a symphony. With the difference that we didn't have to write the melodies. They were written already and all around us. It is because they had found a resonance within us, that we wanted to let them tell their own story and be part of our earthsong. Therefore, with immence gratitude, we thank the authors whom we have quoted.

We thank our friends Dick Birch, Angela Broome, Kathy Gilbert and Martyn Goss for reading the first draft and encouraging us to go on; and more especially Sue Lightfoot for suggesting some excellent poetry and other passages for inclusion. Our anthology might never have left the word-processor without the enthusiastic support of David and Christine Harding who quietly urged us to seek a publisher. Lastly we would like to mention the 'In Other Words' bookshop in Plymouth where we found help with finding books and the answers to many inquiries.

The Compilers and Publishers wish to express their warm appreciation to the holders of Copyright for permission to use quotations in this book. Any omissions or corrections in this matter will gladly be made in any future edition of this book.

AN APOLOGY

We apologise to all those who find sexist language in Earthsong. Wherever possible we have redressed any imbalance.

It is our belief that we must accept our heritage as a blessing, while at the same time actively seek ways of talking about all our relationships which are meaningful and satisfying to both women and men today.

Prologue

Not so long ago we took part in a rescue operation when out walking on Dartmoor. It all happened on a cold spring day. We had hardly set off when we came upon a farmer, a man from the RSPCA and a black and white cow. The cow was lying in a shallow muddy pit which tin miners from a previous century had dug out. The farmer told us that she had calved the day before on the open moor and had stumbled into the pit during the night. Because of her weak condition, she was unable to get out by herself. By now her forefeet were firmly stuck into heavy mud and she was weary and exhausted. How could we walk on? We put our coats on her back and fetched dry bracken to spread over the mud. We calmed and encouraged her as best we could and with the help of a strong rope and a tractor we managed to get her out of the pit. There was relief all round when, at the second attempt she stood up on her own feet. Her calf was already safely in the byre waiting for a drink of warm nourishing milk. It would be a happy reunion. Our rescue operation had taken more than an hour of good hard work. We said goodbye to the farmer and his friend and went on our way.

Dartmoor is the kind of place where we like to meditate a bit and it struck us: wasn't our world rather like this lovely cow and her predicament? The ecological and climatic changes that the demands of an ever increasing human population are helping to bring about can only be dimly visualised. But there is no doubt about it. We are sitting now on our own global "midden". And our own poisonous dirt, stinking greed and ridiculous posturing are slowly chocking us to death. It is red alert time for all the earth.

Two events sparked off our need to write "Earthsong". The cellar of our local OXFAM shop was recently converted into a Third World and Green Resource Centre. Our friend Alan who is a teacher and who helps there on Saturday mornings said to us on one of our visits: 'Why don't you make a green resource pack? - we could do with one'. And so it was that we quietly started to look for material. But our search took a wider perspective when we learned of the latest initiative of the World Council of Churches which has called for a conciliar process on 'Justice, Peace and the Integrity of Creation' asking Christians throughout the world to study these issues and respond out of their experience. We wrote to Geneva for study materials and concentrated our own effort on 'the Integrity of Creation'.

As the material accumulated, we were faced with the problem of how to present it. We took the excellent anthology *'In a Dark Time'* by Nicholas Humphrey and Robert J Lifton as our guide, not in any hope of being able to emulate it but rather as a model of the way that such a collection of material can be organised by the hands of masters.

The Oxford dictionary defines the word integrity as wholeness, soundness, uprightness, honesty. Our friends in Germany study 'die Bewahrung der Schöpfung' while the French talk of 'la sauveguarde de la création'. In the French word 'sauveguarde' are hidden two verbs of action: keep safe and guard. We keep safe and guard something on behalf of someone else. We are entrusted by the past with a responsibility for the future of creation. And God politics are the new Planet politics.

A new territorial imperative comes into being and in the aeons of time, creation is busy taking another leap. A new adventure is already under way.

It is an adventure in which every human being on this planet is called to participate at the political, economic, social and personal level. The exploration outwards will not succeed, however, without a corresponding journey inwards; for this is uncharted country.

It means finding out about our roots; who we are, where we came from, how, and why: of being sure that we set out with sound equipment. It means a recovery, a reconstruction, a making whole of the past in the biological, cultural and spiritual sphere. It means to wonder and meditate on our common past.

Each of us is only part of the story of creation and we now need and want to inhabit a new home: the whole earth. Therefore the whole must sing in us if we are to live in the whole.

This requires a better understanding of how we arrived where we are now in the community of living creatures in all its diversity, and how we are part of it. It is a long journey back in time.

We are also rediscovering the strength of our cultural abundance. Here, a journey to look at our roots is necessary. We must recover the insights of supplanted and long forgotten cultures and take them back to our heart as part of our wealth, blessing and guide.

It means going back to our spiritual roots. For we are all spiritual beings with a capacity - and need to relate, love, transform - to apprehend lasting forms of true beauty, harmony and wholeness. Beings who meditate on the mystery of life. By whatever name we name our God - or give none - God always is the Lifegiver - the Provider, speaking wisdom through the writers of our sacred books, speaking wisdom through poets, mystics and sages, speaking wisdom through the unfolding of all creation itself.

The choice is ours. To be foolish, or to be wise. To long for death, or to cry and give birth. To let Earth die or to love all life with a new might and strength.

And let the Earth sing!

To all you give,
Only from me do you demand.
Descending from your throne,
Smilingly you take to your heart
What out of love I offer you.
What you lay in my hands,
A thousand times enriched
It returns to you.

Rabindranath Tagore: A Flight of Swans.

1

Creation: The Unfolding Story

In the beginning was the Word, and the Word was with God, and the Word was God. All things were made by him; and without him was not anything made that was made. In him was life.

John: 1, 1-4: Revised Version.

The Word is living, being, spirit, all verdant greening, all creativity. This Word manifests itself in every creature.

Hildegarde of Bingen.

Word whose breath is the world-circling atmosphere,
Word that utters the world that turns the wind,
Word that articulates the bird that speeds upon the air,

Word that blazes out the trumpet of the sun,
Whose silence is the violin-music of the stars,
Whose melody is the dawn, and harmony the night,

Word traced in water of lakes, and light on water,
Light on still water, moving water, waterfall
And water colours of cloud, of dew, of spectral rain,

Word inscribed on stone, mountain range upon range of stone,
Word that is fire of the sun and fire within
Order of atoms, crystalline symmetry,
Grammar of five-fold rose and six-fold lily,
Spiral of leaves on a bough, helix of shells,
Rotation of twining plants on axes of darkness and light,

Instinctive wisdom of fish and lion and ram,
Rhythm of generation in flagellate and fern,
Flash of fin, beat of wing, heartbeat, beat of the dance,

Hieroglyph in whose exact precision is defined
Feather and insect-wing, refraction of multiple eyes,
Eyes of the creatures, oh myriadfold vision of the world,

Statement of mystery, how shall we name
A spirit clothed in world, a world made man?

Kathleen Raine: Word made Flesh.

EARTHSONG

Something buried deep in the human psyche compels us to contemplate creation. It is obvious even at a casual glance that the universe is remarkably ordered on all scales. Matter and energy are distributed neither uniformly nor haphazardly, but are organised into coherent identifiable structures, occasionally of great complexity. From whence come the myriads of galaxies, stars and planets. the crystals and clouds, the living organisms? How have they been arranged in such harmonious and ingenious interdependence? The cosmos, its awesome immensity, its rich diversity of forms, and above all its coherent unity, cannot be accepted simply as a brute fact.

The evidence of geology, palaeontology and astronomy suggest that the vast array of forms and structures that populate our world have not always existed, but have emerged over eons of time.

Scientists have recently come to realise that *none* of the objects and systems that make up the physical world we now perceive existed in the beginning. Somehow, all the variety and complexity of the universe has arisen since its origin in an abrupt outburst called the big bang. The modern picture of Genesis is of a cosmos starting out in an utterly featureless state, and then progressing step by step - one may say *unfolding* - to the present state of organised activity.

Paul Davies: The Cosmic Blueprint.

The history of the cosmos
is the history of the struggle of becoming.
When the dim flux of unformed life
struggled, convulsed back and forth upon itself,
and broke at last into light and dark
came into existence as light
came into existence as cold shadow,
then every atom of the cosmos trembled with delight.
Behold, God is born!
He is bright light!
He is pitch dark and cold!

And in the great struggle of intangible chaos
when, at a certain point, a drop of water began to drip
downwards
and a breath of vapour began to wreathe up,
Lo again the shudder of bliss through all the atoms!
Oh, God is born!
Behold, he is born wet!
Look, he hath movement upwards! He spirals!

And so, in the great aeons of accomplishment and debacle
from time to time the wild crying of every electron:
Lo! God is born!

When sapphires cooled out of molten chaos:
See, God is born! He is blue, he is forever blue!
When gold lay shining threading the cooled-off rock:
God is born! God is born! bright yellow and ductile he is born.

When the eggy amoeba emerged out of foam and nowhere
then all the electrons held their breath:
Ah! Ah! Now indeed God is born! He twinkles within.

When from a world of mosses and ferns
at last the narcissus lifted a tuft of five-point stars
and dangled them in the atmosphere,
then every molecule of creation jumped and clapped its hands:
God is born! God is born perfumed and dangling and with a little cup!

Throughout the aeons, as the lizard swirls his tail finer than water,
as the peacock turns to the sun, and could not be more splendid,
as the leopard smites the small calf with a spangled paw, perfect,
the universe trembles: God is born! God is here!

And when at last man stood on two legs and wondered,
and there was a hush of suspence at the core of every electron:
Behold, now very God is born!
God himself is born!
And so we see, God is not
until he is born.
And also we see
there is no end to the birth of God.

D. H. Lawrence: God is Born.

Whence is it that Nature does nothing in vain: and whence arises all that Order and Beauty which we see in the world?

Isaac Newton.

In the beginning the universe erupted spontaneously out of nothing. From a featureless ferment of quantum energy, bubbles of empty space began to inflate at accelerating rate, bootstrapping colossal reserves of energy into existence. This false vacuum, infused with self-created energy, was unstable and began to decay, dumping its energy in the form of heat, filling each bubble with a fireball. Inflation ceased, but the big bang was started. The time was 10^{-32}s.

In the old classical physics, the science of mechanics exemplified the rigid control of causality. The activity of every particle, each twist and turn, was considered to be legislated in detail by the laws of motion... the entire universe was supposed to be regulated in every minute detail by the existing pattern of activity, like gigantic clockwork. It was this all-embracing, utterly dependable causality that prompted Pierre Laplace's claim about a powerful calculator being able to compute the entire history and destiny of the cosmos from the operation of mechanical laws. The universe, according to this view, is for ever unfolding along a pre-ordained pathway.

Quantum physics wrecked the orderly, yet sterile Laplacian scheme. Physicists learned that at the atomic level matter and motion are vague and unpredictable. Particles can behave erratically, rebelling against rigidly prescribed motions, turning up in unexpected places without discernable reason and even appearing and disappearing without warning.

Causality is not completely absent in the quantum realm, but it is faltering and ambiguous... The quantum world is not, therefore, linked by a tight network of causal influences, but more by a pandemonium of loosely obeyed commands and suggestions.

Paul Davies: Superforce.

Subatomic particles forever partake in this unceasing dance of annihilation and creation. In fact, subatomic particles *are* this unceasing dance of annihilation and creation...

Philosophically the 20th Century discovery of quantum physics with all its psychedelic implications is not new. It is very similar to the way that much of the earth's population view their reality...

Not only do we influence our reality, but, in some way we actually create it...

John Wheeler, a well-known physicist at Princeton, wrote: 'May the universe in some strange sense be "brought into being" by the participation of those who participate? The vital act is the act of participation. "Participator" is the incontrovertible new concept given by quantum mechanics. It strikes down the term "observer" of classical theory, the man who stands behind the thick glass wall and watches what goes on without taking part. It can't be done, quantum mechanics says.'

It leads to the possibility that our reality is what we choose to make it.

The Wu Li Masters know that physicists are doing more than "discovering the endless diversity of nature". They are dancing with Kali, The Divine Mother of Hindu Mythology.

"Who are the dancers and who the dance? They have no attributes other than the dance".

"What is 'they'?"

"The things that dance, the dancers..."

Gary Zukav: The Dancing Wu Li Masters.

ooooooooooo

Science has been dominated for several centuries by the Newtonian paradigm which treats the universe as a mechanism, ultimately reducible to the behaviour of individual particles under the control of deterministic forces. According to this view time is merely a parameter; there is no real change or evolution, only the rearrangement of particles. The laws of thermodynamics reintroduced the notion of flux or change, but the reconciliation of the Newtonian and thermodynamic paradigms led only to the second law, which insists that all change is part of the inexorable decay and degeneration of the cosmos, culminating in heat death.

The emerging paradigm, by contrast, recognises that the collective and holistic properties of physical systems can display new and unforeseen modes of behaviour that are not captured by the Newtonian and thermodynamic approaches. There arises the possibility of *self-organisation*, in which systems suddenly and spontaneously leap into more elaborate forms. These forms are characterized by greater complexity, by cooperative behaviour and global coherence, by the appearence of spatial patterns and temporal rhythms, and by general unpredictability of their final forms...

Above all, the new paradigm transforms our view of time. Physical systems can display unidirectional change in the direction of *progress* rather than decay. The universe is revealed in a new, more inspiring light, unfolding from its primitive beginnings and progressing step by step to ever more elaborate and complex states.

Paul Davies: Cosmic Blueprint.

ooooooooooo

What makes different letters separate from one another is precisely what makes it possible for them to be put together in a word. Similarly, it is what causes separations between words that puts the words together to produce sentences. So, in the end, it is in this interplay between different levels that the meaning of the whole seems to take place. And if we ask ourselves where we could locate the meaning of language, then we come up with the strange but suggestive idea that it is to be found ... in the space between the letters.

Henri Atlan.

I do not paint things but the relationship between them.

Henri Matisse.

[The] most complex and all-embracing of the levels in the hierarchies of 'systems' [is] the complex of nature-man-and-God. For when human beings are exercising themselves in their God-directed and worshipping activities they are operating at a level in the hierarchy of complexity which is more intricate and cross-related than any of those that arise in the natural and social sciences... For in his.. God-related activities man utilises every facet of his total being: his solitary, inner self-consciousness; his interaction with other people at the most personal level; his interaction with nature and the universe; and his relation to what he regards as ultimate. For religion is about the ultimate meaning that a person finds in his or her relation with all-that-is.

Arthur Peacocke: God and the New Biology.

It seems that a random event - a coming together of atoms in a particular pattern or the mutation of a gene - is the source of novelty in the evolution of complex systems. Such new possibilities would vanish again were they not selectively perpetuated by competitive processes acting in an environment of lawful necessity. Without chance there would be no change and development; without necessity there would be no preservation and selection... Instead of seeing chance as an indication of the purposelessness and futility of the world, I was deeply moved by the thought of the astonishing fruitfulness that [is] revealed inherent in the laws of physics. These basic laws are just Maxwell's equations (to express the forces of electromagnetism controlling the larger-scale structure of matter) and the Schrödinger equation (to express the quantum theory necessary for molecular dynamics). I could literally write them down on the back of an envelope. Yet the fact that they can have such remarkable consequences as you and me speaks of the amazing potentiality contained in their structure. From this point of view the action of chance is to explore and realise that inherent fruitfulness. Arthur Peacocke wrote: 'This role of chance is what one would expect of the universe were it so organised as to be able to explore all potential forms of the organisation of matter (both living and non-living) which it contains.

John Polkinghorn: One World.

Such a world is a world of orderliness but not of clockwork regularity, of potentiality without predictability, endowed with an assurance of development but with a certain openness as to its actual form. It is inevitably a world with ragged edges, where order and disorder interlace with each other and where the exploration of possibility by chance will lead not only to the evolution of systems of increasing complexity, endowed with new possibilities, but also to the evolution of systems imperfectly formed and malfunctioning. The former superior entities will earn the epithet 'successful' by their survival in the competition for constituent resources; the latter inferior entities will disappear from the evolving scene. It is just such a world that we live in.

John Polkinghorn: Science and Creation.

Time is creation. The future is just not *there*.

Ilya Prigogine.

The extravagant gesture is the very stuff of creation. After the one extravagant gesture of creation in the first place, the universe has continued to deal exclusively in extravagances, flinging intricacies and colossi down aeons of emptiness, heaping profusions on profligacies with ever fresh vigor. The whole show has been on fire from the word go!

Annie Dillard: Pilgrim at Tinker Creek.

Outside Time the Consciousness of God exists.
In that Consciousness
is a thought
of such intensity that within it
all and everything
conceivable and inconceivable,
imaginable and unimaginable,
possible and impossible
is contained.
That thought is uttered
and from the vibrations of that sound
from the resonance of that Word,
from what scientists call
'The Big Bang',
the multitudinous forms of being are spreading
in ever increasing circles.

Our being is the expression of God's thought.
We contain the love of God and God contains us
and as we unfold on earth

through shell creature,
fish-form,
reptile,
bird
and mammal -
we are learning
step by step
what that containment means.

The circles are still widening -
still evolving the mighty concept -
the magnificent Idea.
Six days,
Seven...
a million years,
a thousand million...
the count is nothing,
the Being - All.
Praise be to our great God
and the Word that resonates
in our hearts still.
May we not separate ourselves in arrogance
from the Great Work
for we know the sound of the Word
but not its full meaning.

Moyra Caldecott (abridged).

The activity of God in creation must be precarious. It must proceed by no assured programme. Its progress, like every progress in love, must be an angular progress - in which every step is a precarious step into the unknown... If the creation is the work of love, than its shape cannot be predetermined by the Creator, nor its triumph foreknown; it is the realisation of vision, but of vision which is discovered only through its own realization: all faith in its triumph is neither more nor less than faith in the Creator Himself - faith that He will not cease from His handiwork nor abandon the object of His love.

W H Vanstone: Love's Endeavour, Love's Expense.

A creation-centered spirituality is cosmic. It is open, seeking, and explorative of the cosmos within the human person and all creatures and of the cosmos without, the spaces between creatures that unite us all. The more and more one sinks into our cosmic existence the more fully one realises the truth that there does not exist an inside and an outside cosmos but rather one cosmos: we are in the cosmos and the cosmos is in us. As John Muir put it, 'When we try to pick out anything by itself, we find it hitched to everything else in the Universe... The whole wilderness is unity and interrelation is alive and familiar.' All things are interrelated because all things are microcosms of a macrocosm. And it is all in motion, it is all *en route*, it is all moving, vibrant, dancing, and full of surprises. It is all a blessing, an ongoing and fertile blessing with a holy, salvic history of about twenty billion years.

Matthew Fox: Original Blessing.

ϖϖϖϖϖϖϖ

I am the power that tears apart the stars
and folds them into galaxies.
I call the buds of flowers
to bloom in the delicate dawn.
And I am the power in the leopard's limbs,
and the dandelioned wind.
I shake the earth apart in stormèd fire,
and spill my life-blood upon the Earth
each Spring,
taking it back again from withered leaves
which fall upon my bosom
in the year's close.
I weave the webbéd lace of spider's deeds
and hear crystals grow
in ice-locked cliffs, long abandoned.
I dance in the heavens, playing with the stars,
and garland the sun with planets,
setting the Earth's jewel in the centre of my head.

I dwell in desert drifted sands
and in the rhythm of the seas,
beneath the molten-angered rocks.
And in a child's eyes.
I soar in the flight of the snow-birds,
and creep within the burrows of the Earth.
I vibrate in the music of the stars,
and in the silence of the worlds
long dead.
All creation is my being.
And if you would cease your search
of the Earth's ends
and the distant skies
and turn within,
you would see me vibrating in your heart
with shining Love,
as I shine in the hearts
of all men.
Go there,
and you will see me in everything.

Mala Mason: Shivoham.

ϖϖϖϖϖϖϖ

Must we not say that this 'Creation outside God' exists simultaneously *in* God, in the space which God has made for it in his Omnipresence? Has God not therefore created the world 'in himself', giving it time *in* his eternity, finitude *in* his infinity, space *in* his omnipresence and freedom *in* his selfless love?

Jürgen Moltmann: The Trinity and the Kingdom of God.

'The world' is not simply something that can be joined to 'God' by the word 'and', as in traditional theistic discourse, but that it is in God and God is in it....there is a coinherence between God and the universe which overcomes the duality without denying the diversity'.

John Robinson: Exploration into God.

O Holy Spirit,
You are the mighty way in which every
thing that is in the heavens,
on the earth, and under the earth,
is penetrated with connectedness,
is penetrated with relatedness.

Hildegarde of Bingen.

The world is a-building. This is the basic truth which first must be understood so thoroughly that it becomes an habitual and as it were natural springboard for our thinking. At first sight, beings and their destinies might seem to us to be scattered haphazard or at least in an arbitrary fashion over the face of the earth; we could very easily suppose that each of us might *equally* have been born earlier or later, at this place or that, happier or more ill-starred, as though the universe from the beginning to the end of its history formed in space-time a sort of vast flower-bed in which the flowers could be changed at the whim of the gardener. But this idea is surely untenable. The more one reflects, with the help of all that science, philosophy and religion can teach us, each in its own field, the more one comes to realise that the world should be likened not to a bundle of elements artificially held together but rather some organic system animated by a broad movement of development which is proper to itself. As the centuries go by it seems that a comprehensive plan is indeed slowly being carried out around us. A process is at work in the universe, an issue is at stake, which can best be compared with the process of gestation and birth; the birth of that spiritual reality which is formed by souls and by such material reality as their existence involves. Laboriously, through and thanks to the activity of mankind, the new earth is being formed and purified and is taking on definition and clarity. No, we are not like the cut flowers that make up a bouquet: we are like the leaves and buds of a great tree on which everything appears at its proper time and place as required and determined by the good of the whole.

Pierre Teilhard de Chardin: Hymn of The Universe.

You are a child of the universe, no less than the trees & the stars, you have a right to be here. And whether or not it is clear to you, no doubt the universe is unfolding as it should.

From a document dated 1692, found in Old St Paul's Church, Baltimore.

Man tread softly on the Earth
What looks like dust
Is also the stuff of which galaxies are made.

The green of Earth's great trees and simple grasses
Is the same music played in red
Throughout our trunks and limbs.

The first eye broadcast thought

Function is the eye dust
Fragrance is the flower's eye.
The furred and feathered eye is freedom.
If we cannot see that dust looks back at us
If we do not see Mind in the flower's scent
If we will not see thought in the animal
It is because we bind our eyes
To stay Evolution's seeing.

O blessed Earth. O patient Earth
We struggle upward to the sun
Forgetting what as dust we knew
Forgetting what as flowers we saw
Forgetting what we as animals are
Forgetting humanness is synthesis
Of dust, flower, animal and something more.

O Earth, living, breathing, thinking Earth
On the day we treasure you
As you have treasured us
Humanness is born.

And throughout all Light
A Radiance leaps from star to star
Singing: A Son is born
HUMANITY.

Evelyn Nolt: The Glory which is Earth.

EARTHSONG

The human person
is the form
and the fullness
of creation.

In humankind
God brings to fullness all his creation.

God created humankind,
so that humankind
might cultivate the earthly
and thereby
create the heavenly.

Human kind should be the banner of divinity.

With nature's help,
humankind can set into creation
all that is necessary and life sustaining.

God's majesty is glorified
in the manifestation of every manner
of nature's fruitfulness.

This is possible,
possible through the right and holy
utilization of the earth,
the earth in which humankind has its source.

The sum total of heaven and earth,
everything in nature,
is thus won to use and purpose.

It becomes a temple and altar
for the service of God.

Hildegarde of Bingen.

C. G. Jung has written that there are two ways to lose your soul. One of these is to worship a god outside you. If he is correct, then a lot of churchgoers in the West have been losing their souls for generations to the extent that they have attended religious events where prayer is addressed to a God outside. The idea that God is 'out there' is probably the ultimate dualism, divorcing as it does God and humanity and reducing religion to a childish state of pleasing or pleading with a God 'out there'. All theism sets up a model or paradigm of people here and God out there. All theisms are about subject/object relationships with God. The Newtonian theism that posited a clockmaker God who wound up the universe and sat back, found its logical conclusion in Laplace's statement that he had no need in his scientific system for such a God. But this agnosticism and eventual atheism finds its logical antecedents in religious theism itself, which kills God and the soul alike by preaching a God 'out there'.

What is the solution to the killing of God and the loss of human soul? It is our moving from theism to panentheism. Now panentheism is not pantheism. Pantheism, which is a declared heresy because it robs God of Transcendence, states that 'everything is God and God is everything'. Panentheism, on the other hand is altogether orthodox and very fit for orthopraxis as well, for it slips in the little Greek word *en* and thus means, 'God is in everything and everything is in God'... Panentheism is desperately needed by individuals and religious institutions today. It is the way the creation-centered tradition of spirituality experiences God... Panentheism is a way of seeing the world sacramentally. Indeed ... in the creation-centered tradition the primary sacrament is creation itself - which includes every person and being who lives. Other sacraments derive their fruitful and creative power from this primary sacrament.

Matthew Fox: Original Blessing.

God orders the universe, according to panentheism, by taking into his own life all the currents of feelings of existence. He is the most irresistable of influences precisely because he is himself the most open to influence. In the depths of their hearts all creatures (even those able to 'rebel' against him) defer to God because they sense him as the one who alone is adequately moved by what moves them. He alone not only knows but feels (the only adequate knowledge where feeling is concerned) how they feel, and he finds his own joy in sharing their lives, lived according to their own free decisions not fully anticipated by any detailed plan of his own.... In this vision of a deity who is not a supreme autocrat, but a universal agent of 'persuasion', whose 'power' is the worship he 'inspires', that is, flows from the intrinsic appeal of his infinitely sensitive and tolerant relativity, by which all things are kept moving in orderly togetherness, we may find help in facing our task today.

Charles Hartshorne: The Divine Relativity.

God is not nowhere but everywhere. He is infinitely present, not infinitely absent. He is not disembodied in any negative sense. There is no body which is not His body. That sounds like 'pantheism' and Christians take fright. We are not allowed to say that God *is* the universe or that the universe *is* God. If we suggest anything of the kind we are falling into idolatry or nonsense or both. But some Christian thinkers lately have taken hold of another technical term, 'pan-en-theism', 'all-in-God-ism', offered as a way of responsibly relating God to everything there is.

God is much more than the physical universe but there is no need to think of Him as *dis*embodied. As Creator and Upholder of all things He is totally 'in touch' with everything... We are both powerful, and vulnerable, through our separate bodies; and we may imagine that God is powerful, and vulnerable, through every creature.

Helen Oppenheimer: Looking Before and After.

Between God and our soul there is neither wrath nor forgiveness, because there is no between.

Julian of Norwich.

There is involved in Christian faith a claim about reality, inherited from the prophets and vindicated in Jesus. This is the claim that history can, must and will be related to the kingdom and community of God. But this is not an invitation to, or a licence for, any form of historicism. That is to say it does not admit or encourage the belief that history has one clear pattern or direction which is discernable, achievable or inevitable. To clamp a pattern on history or to claim that we have the esoteric knowledge which gives us the vital clue to history is to misunderstand both the freedom of God and the God of freedom and so to misunderstand the human predicament and the human condition. Our lives in history are not the substance of the kingdom of God, only the material for it.

What is involved here is a profound question about our understanding of God. God is not the mastermind of a vast construction activity, planned in computerised fashion from the beginning and moving on inevitably to a predetermined and preconceived end. He...is much more like a master artist... This mysterious artist is committed in passion, righteousness and holiness to an infinite creative activity, launched by love, and seeking, making and feeling ways forward by freedom and in freedom. The movement and the struggle is through tremendous risks, to a fulfilment of a commitment, a vision and a hope which will establish a community and kingdom commensurate with the initial love, the consequent cost and the subsequent promise. Nothing is certain but everything is possible. Such committed and constructive openness is the basic condition of freedom and love.

David Jenkins: God, Politics and the Future.

Within creation there is autonomy and within that autonomy there is given to us, who are made in God's image, a real measure of freedom. That is the limited extent of our power. Yes, we have power. We may not like it. We may prefer to ascribe it to God. But it is ours. We are, within the complex limitations of this created order, plenipotentiaries. Limited only - yet substantially - by our total interdependence with the rest of creation and by our inherited past. We are knit into a continuum not of our own individual choosing. Within that framework we are free.

In consequence, the kind of prayer that tells God what to do is a rejection of our true role, a refusal to accept responsibility. It is not God who starts or ends wars. We do. God does not feed hungry children or let them starve. God does not rule or overrule. The world is not his puppet theatre... But, even knowing that, we need not escape into the role of God's publicity agent. More is wrought by the mystery of the prayer of a loving heart than our reason can grasp... And, as mysteriously as our prayer is part of reality, so God, present, living, suffering, and dying, is part of that reality too; immanent and transcendant. But not, not, not a God at the controls.

Paul Oestreicher: The Double Cross.

Each year when Good Friday and Easter Sunday approach us our thoughts turn toward the great drama of redemption, culminating in the pictures of the Cross and Resurrection. Who is redeemed? Some men alone; or mankind, including all nations; or the world, everything that is created, including nature, the stars and the clouds, the winds and the oceans, the stones and the plants, the animals and our own bodies? The bible speaks again and again of the salvation of the world, as it speaks of the creation of the world... And world means nature as well as man.

Paul Tillich: The Shaking of the Foundations.

Inasmuch as God is the father, I am the child. I have not emerged fully from the autistic wish for omniscience and omnipotence. I have not yet acquired the objectivity to realise my limitations as a human being, my ignorance, my helplessness. I still claim, like a child, that there must be a father who rescues me, who watches me, who punishes me, a father who likes me when I am obedient, who is flattered by my praise and angry because of my disobedience... The truly religious person, if he follows the essence of the monotheistic idea, does not pray for anything, does not expect anything from God; he does not love God as a child loves his father or his mother; he has acquired the humility of sensing his limitations to the degree of knowing that he knows nothing about God.

Erich Fromm: The Art of Loving.

ꝏꝏꝏꝏꝏꝏ

So our coming of age forces us to a true recognition of our situation *vis a vis* God. God is teaching us that we must live as men who can get along very well without him. The God who is with us is the God who forsakes us. The God who makes us live in this world without using him as a working hypothesis is the God before whom we are ever standing. Before God and with him we live without God. God allows himself to be edged out of this world and on to the cross. God is weak and powerless in this world, and that is exactly the way, the only way, in which he can be with us and help us.

Dietrich Bonhoeffer: Letters & Papers from Prison.

ꝏꝏꝏꝏꝏꝏ

Nothing is demanded of you - no idea of God, and no goodness in yourselves, not your being religious, not your being Christian, not your being wise, and not your being moral. What is asked is only your being open and willing to accept what is given to you, the New Being, the being of love and justice and truth, as is manifest in Him whose yoke is easy and whose burden is light.

Paul Tillich: The Shaking of the Foundations.

ꝏꝏꝏꝏꝏꝏ

God, in all that is most living and incarnate in Him, is not far away from us, altogether apart from the world we see, touch, hear, smell and taste about us. Rather He awaits us at every instant of our action, in the work of the moment. There is a sense in which He is at the tip of my pen, my spade, my brush, my needle - of my heart and of my thought. By pressing the stroke, the line, or the stitch, on which I am engaged, to its ultimate natural finish, I shall lay hold of the last end towards which my innermost will tends... Try, with God's help, to perceive the connection - even physical and natural - which binds your labour with the building of the Kingdom of Heaven; try to realise that heaven itself smiles upon you and through your works, draws you to itself; then, as you leave church for the noisy streets, you will remain with only one feeling, that of continuing to immerse yourself in God.

Pierre Teilhard de Chardin: Le Milieu Divin.

ꝏꝏꝏꝏꝏꝏ

Everything is relative. Every Commandment that ever issued out of the mouth of God or man is strictly relative; adhering to the particular time, place and circumstances...

For the relatedness and interrelatedness of all things flows and changes and trembles like a stream...

If we think about it, we find that our life *consists in* this achievement of a pure relationship between ourselves and the living universe around us. This is how I 'save my soul' by accomplishing a pure relationship between me and another person, me and other people, me and a nation, me and the race of men, me and the animals, me and the trees and flowers, me and the earth, me and the skies and sun and the stars, me and the moon: an infinity of pure relations, big and little, like the stars of the sky: that makes our eternity, for each one of us, me and the timber I am sawing, the lines of force I follow; me and the dough I knead into bread, me and the very motion with which I write, me and the bit of gold I have got. This, if we knew it, is our life and our eternity: the subtle, perfected relation between me and my whole circumambient universe.

And morality is that delicate, for ever changing and trembling balance between me and my circumambient universe, which preceeds and accompanies a true relatedness.

D. H. Lawrence: Reflections on the Death of a Porcupine.

God's silence is mysterious. Sometimes it fills us with fright and paralyses us in the face of the devils who squeeze out the life of the people. But without this silence of God we can't become men and women. When God speaks all the time, people become deaf. They don't hear the cry of the poor and of those who suffer. They become dull; they no longer walk and hope. They don't dare to do anything. They no longer endure. God remains silent so that men and women may speak, protest, and struggle. God remains silent so that people may become really people.

Elsa Tamez: A Letter to Job. Quoted in 'Encounters' 1988.

We are always wanting to pin God down by getting things cut and dried and decisive. God is always wanting to set us free to share in the mystery and the suffering of creation, freedom and redemption. God undertook the cross when he undertook creation. We - and especially religious people organised into churches - are always trying to limit the risk, curtail the openness, contract the freedom and avoid the commitment of faith which is falling into the risk and abyss of love.

David Jenkins: God, Miracle and the Church of England.

Here is the adventure. The hero
a trailing dot something like a tadpole
lolling at ease in a comfy lagoon.

The tide rising. A chill sea
creeping towards him. A swarm of basking shadows
clouding the water

and now the wind rising stirs in him
a queasy optimism, a vague big *Something*.
The waves are colder, more insistent

sharpening their cutting edges. A madness
has seized his companions for they've turned
tails towards the current and are swimming

furiously upriver like salmon in grim formation.
The Something roars to life inside him.
He knows himself Sperm, a need, a light-streak....

In the mind of God
which is not yet awakened, radiance:
light inseparable from darkness;

the face of the abyss, which is death
covered by darkness: death, not yet discovered
and darkness itself, not yet manifest.

A mighty wind, which is the spirit of God
moving on the waters
which are life, unmanifest;

earth inseparable from water: matter, unmanifest,
the waters above not yet separated
from the waters below: spirit, not yet divided;

time uncreated, space, the finite and infinite
unseparated. And God said
Let there be light, and there was light:

The dawning of conciousness
in the mind of God, light separated from
the great darkness which is the unconscious, manifest.

So the first separation, the beginning of polarity,
and with it, evening and morning
the dawn of time.

Time manifest and within it
the first creation: space divided into form:
the vault of heaven:

the waters above separated
from the waters below: Spirit divided from itself
by the vault of heaven which is

the vault of the skull.
And so to earth.

Earth. Below the blue vault of heaven
the waters gathered:
land and sea, spirit and flesh, duality

multiplying, and the earth made fruitful:
a garden of plants bearing seed, an orchard with fruit
each bearing seed fruitful, paradise which is

the meaning of garden.
So God turned again to heaven. In the great vault
he set the two great lights:

Sun, which is consciousness and with it
day, the finite, visible; Moon which is of itself
darkness and therefore has no clear name:

Intuition, Emotion, Dream
rough nicknames, the glimpsed,
reflected light to illuminate darkness

in the canopy of heaven
and with it stars, the infinite suns
painted on the vault which is itself, infinite.

Sperm is calling, swimming like an astronaut
through the silky folds of the universe.
He turns his egg-shaped head this way and that.

He lashes with his whiplash tail.
Her beauty shines out of the darkness
a radiant planet, filling the sky.

He swims towards her - she is growing
larger each second. He dives into her head first
vanishes wriggling in swirling cloud.

His queer spiral markings lock
indelibly with hers. It is finished.
His molecule chains unhook and float away.

It is possible to tell this story
ten thousand times without understanding it.
When old men, staring into flames

or jewel thieves rummaging in mythology
chart its progress
or scientists with their microscopic cameras

enter closer and closer into mystery
they gather details.
We may not see creation with our own eyes

EARTHSONG

or mechanical eyes or the wide dreaming eyes
of the mind.
Eggs are everywhere planted, eaten, multiplying

but their secret remains closed.
In my body which is the universe, an egg
is alive. I name it child.

Jeni Couzyn: Life by Drowning.

2

The Earth's Vital Statistics

Equatorial radius	= 6378.164 Km
Polar radius	= 6356.779 Km
Equatorial circumference	= 40,075.24 Km
Meridional circumference	= 40,008.08 Km
Mass	= 5.967×10^{24} Kg
Volume	= 1.0832×10^{27} cm^3
Average density	= 5.518 g cm^{-3}
Land area	= 1.49×10^{18} cm^2
Ocean area	= 3.61×10^{18} cm^2
Average land elevation	= 860 m
Average ocean depth	= 3900 m

Surface gravity	= 980.665 cm s^{-2}
Velocity of rotation at equator	= 1674 Km hr^{-1}
Mean velocity of orbit around sun	= 107,208 Km hr^{-1}
Increase in day length	= 0.0015 s $century^{-1}$
Average rate of movement of continents	= 2 cm/y

TIME & AGE

Age of the Earth	= 4.55	thousand million years
Oldest rocks	= 3.55	thousand million years
Bacteria, Blue-Green Algae	= 3	thousand million years
Sponges, Algae, Fungi	= 2	thousand million years
Coelenterates, Flatworms Higher Plants	= 1 to 400	thousand million million years
Arthropods, Vertebrates	= 600 to 450	million million years
Mammals, Birds	= 150	million years
Humankind	= 50	thousand years

UNIVERSAL CONSTANTS

Velocity of light	= 2.9979250×10^{10} cm sec^{-1}
Gravitation constant	= 6.670×10^{-8} dyn cm^{2} g^{-2}
Plank constant	= 6.62620×10^{-27} erg s
Schrödinger constant	= 1.63817×10^{27} erg^{-1} cm^{2}
Electron charge	= 4.80325×10^{-10} ESU
Mass of electron	= 9.10956×10^{-28} g
Radius of electron	= 2.81794×10^{-13} cm
Mass of proton	= 1.672661×10^{-24} g
Radius of first Bohr orbit	= 0.5291775×10^{-8} cm
Frequency of first Bohr orbit	= 6.5797×10^{15} s^{-1}
Boltzman constant	= 1.38062×10^{-16} erg deg^{-1}
Gas constant	= 8.3143×10^{7} erg deg^{-1} mole^{-1}
Avogadro number	= 6.02217×10^{23}

3

Dance, dance wherever you may be!

Unite and unite and let us all unite,
For summer is a-come unto day;
And whither we are going we will all unite,
In the merry morning of May.

Traditional: May-day Festival, Padstow, Cornwall.

Before the High and Far-Off Times, O my Best Beloved, came the Time of the Very Beginnings; and that was in the days when the Eldest Magician was getting Things ready. First he got the Earth ready; then he got the sea ready; and then he told all the Animals that they could come out and play. And the animals said, 'O Eldest Magician, what shall we play at?' and he said, 'I will show you.' He took the Elephant - All-the-Elephant-there-was - and said, 'Play at being an Elephant,' and All-the-Elephant-there-was played...

Rudyard Kipling: Just So Stories.

And joy is everywhere; it is in the earth's green covering of grass; in the blue serenity of the sky; in the reckless exuberance of spring; in the severe abstinence of grey winter; in the living flesh that animates our bodily frame; in the perfect poise of the human figure, noble and upright; in living; in the exercise of all our powers; in the acquisition of knowledge; in fighting evils; in dying for gains we never can share. Joy is there everywhere; it is superfluous, unnecessary; nay, it very often contradicts the most peremptory behests of necessity. It exists to show that the bonds of law can only be explained by love; they are like body and soul. Joy is the realisation of the truth of oneness, the oneness of our soul with the world and of the world-soul with the supreme lover.

Rabindranath Tagore: Gitanjali.

EARTHSONG

"Today I am completely happy."
That took some risk to say aloud.
I left them walking, ran
to clasp the nearest tree
"Touch wood!", I cried.

Heather Harrison: Roots Beneath the Pavement.

I was utterly alone with the sun and the earth. Lying down on the grass, I spoke in my soul to the earth, the sun, the air, and the distant sea far beyond sight. I thought of the earth's firmness - I felt it bear me up; through the grassy couch there came an influence as if I could feel the great earth speaking to me. I thought of the wandering air - its pureness, which is its beauty; the air touched me and gave me something of itself. I spoke to the sea: though so far, in my mind I saw it, green at the rim of the earth and blue in deeper ocean; I desired to have its strength, its mystery and glory. Then I addressed the sun, desiring the soul equivalent of his light and brilliance, his endurance and unwearied race. I turned to the blue heaven over, gazing into its depth, inhaling its exquisite colour and sweetness. The rich blue of the unattainable flower of the sky drew my soul towards it, and there it rested, for pure colour is rest of the heart. By all these I prayed...

Through every grass blade in the thousand, thousand grasses; through the million leaves, veined and edge cut, on bush and tree; through the song-notes and the marked feathers of the birds; through the insects' hum and the colour of the butterflies; through the soft warm air, the flocks of clouds dissolving - I used them all for prayer... I prayed with the glowing clouds of sunset and the soft light of the first star coming through the violet sky. At night now with the stars... with the morning star, the light-bringer...

All the glory of the sunrise filled me with broader and furnace-like vehemence of prayer. Thus I might have the deepest soul-life, deeper far than all this greatness of the visible universe and even of the invisible; that I might have a fullness of soul till now unknown, and utterly beyond my own conception.

Richard Jeffries, The Story of my Heart. 1883.

Forget not that the earth
delights to feel your bare feet
and the winds long to play with your hair.

Kahlil Gibran: The Prophet.

Four horses;
My team,
Eager, restless
Waiting;
Waiting to lurch forward
At my command.
Ready, we're off.
Trot, canter, gallop,
It's a mad gallop.
Running furiously.
My hair flowing
Likes the manes
Of my team
Beautiful.
The wind
Makes my cheeks
Pale.
My cloak flows;
Out behind
My belt useless
Not able to cope
With my flapping tunic.
No other sound
Except the continual
Pulse in my ears
In time with
My horses hoofs,
Thud, thud, thud,
I feel weightless
Weightless.
Getting slower
Slower
Gallop, canter, trot.... Finish.

Helen Colebrook: Exhilaration.

Light, my light, the world-filling light, the eye-kissing light, heart-sweetening light!

Ah, the light dances, my darling, at the centre of my life; the light strikes, my darling, the chords of my love; the sky opens, the wind runs wild, laughter passes over the earth.

The butterflies spread their sails on the sea of light, lillies and jasmines surge up on the crest of the waves of light.

The light is shattered into gold on every cloud, my darling, and it scatters gems in profusion.

Mirth spreads from leaf to leaf, my darling, and gladness without measure. The heaven's river has drowned its banks and the flood of joy is abroad.

Rabindranath Tagore: Gitanjali.

EARTHSONG

And the sea the sea crimson sometimes like fire and the glorious sunsets and the figtrees in the Alameda gardens YES and all the queer little streets and pink and blue and yellow houses and rosegardens and the jasmine and geraniums and cactuses and Gibraltar as a girl where I was a flower of the mountain YES when I put the rose in my hair like the Andalusian girls used or shall I wear a red YES and how he kissed me under the moorish wall and I asked him with my eyes to ask again YES and then he asked me would I YES to say YES my mountain flower and first I put my arms around him YES and drew him down to me YES and his heart was going like mad and YES I said YES I will YES.

James Joyce: Ulysses.

ꝏꝏꝏꝏꝏꝏ

To live with a deep awareness of the elemental Oneness of all creation is to partake of "God consciousness." Such experiental, rather than merely intellectual, awareness of the profound connectedness is what I hold to be the true meaning of being in "a state of grace." Awe at the intricate wonders of creation and celebration of the cosmic unfolding are the roots of worship.

Charlene Spretnak: The Spiritual Dimension of Green Politics.

ꝏꝏꝏꝏꝏꝏ

Most high, all powerful, all good Lord!
All praise is yours, all glory, all honour and blessing.
To you, alone, Most High, do they belong.
No mortal lips are worthy
To pronounce your name.
All praise be yours, my Lord, through all that you have made,
And first my Lord Brother Sun,
Who brings the day; and light you give to us through him.
How beautiful is he, how radiant in all his splendour!
Of you, most high, he bears the likeness.
All praise be yours, my Lord, Through Sister Moon and Stars;
In the heavens you have made them, bright
And precious and fair.
All praise be yours, my Lord, through brothers Wind and Air,
And fair and stormy, all the weather's moods,
By which you cherish all that you have made.
All praise be yours, my Lord, through the Sister Water,
So useful, lowly, precious and pure.
All praise be yours, my Lord, through Brother Fire,
Through whom you brighten up the night.
How beautiful he is, how gay! Full of power and strength.
All praise be yours, my Lord, through Sister Earth, my mother
Who feeds us in her sovereignty and produces
Various fruits with coloured flowers and herbs.

St Francis of Assisi.

ꝏꝏꝏꝏꝏꝏ

O ye Heavens, bless ye the Lord:
praise him, and magnify him for ever

O ye sun and moon, bless ye the Lord:
praise him, and magnify him for ever.

O ye stars of heaven, bless ye the Lord:
praise him, and magnify him for ever.

O ye winds of God, bless ye the Lord:
praise him, and magnify him for ever.

O ye winter and summer, bless ye the Lord:
praise him, and magnify him for ever.

O ye ice and snow, bless ye the Lord:
praise him, and magnify him for ever.

O ye nights and days, bless ye the Lord:
praise him, and magnify him for ever.

O ye light and darkness, bless ye the Lord:
praise him, and magnify him for ever.

O let the earth praise the Lord:
yea, let it praise him, and magnify him for ever.

O ye mountains and hills, bless ye the Lord:
praise him, and magnify him for ever.

O all ye green things upon the earth, bless ye the Lord:
praise him, and magnify him for ever.

O ye seas and floods, bless ye the Lord:
praise him, and magnify him for ever.

O ye whales and all that move in the waters, bless ye the Lord:
praise him, and magnify him for ever.

O all ye fowls of the air, bless ye the Lord:
praise him, and magnify him for ever.

O all ye beasts and cattle, bless ye the Lord:
praise him, and magnify him for ever.

O ye children of men, bless ye the Lord:
praise him, and magnify him for ever.

O let the earth bless the lord:
yea let it praise him and magnify him forever.

The Book of Common Prayer: Benedicite, Omnia Opera (abridged).

EARTHSONG

O be joyful in the Lord all ye lands: serve the Lord with gladness, and come before his presence with a song.

Be ye sure that the Lord he is God: it is he that hath made us, and not we ourselves; we are his people, and the sheep of his pasture.

O go your way into his gates with thanksgiving, and into his courts with praise: be thankful unto him, and speak good of his name.

For the Lord is gracious, his mercy is everlasting: and his truth endureth from generation to generation.

Psalm 100: Jubilate Deo: The Book of Common Prayer.

ꝏꝏꝏꝏꝏꝏ

I believe, O God of all gods,
That Thou art the eternal Father of life;
I believe, O God of all gods,
That Thou art the eternal Father of love

I believe, O God of all gods,
That Thou art the eternal Father of the saints;
I believe, O God of all gods,
That Thou art the eternal Father of each one.

I believe, O God of all gods,
That Thou art the eternal Father of mankind;
I believe, O God of all gods,
That Thou art the eternal Father of the world.

I believe, O Lord and God of the peoples,
That Thou art the creator of the high heavens,
That Thou art the creator of the skies above,
That Thou are the creator of the oceans below.

I believe, O Lord and God of the peoples,
That Thou art He Who created my soul and set its warp.

Who created my body from dust and from ashes,
Who gave my body breath, and to my soul its possesion.

Father, bless to me my body,
Father, bless to me my soul,
Father, bless to me my life,
Father, bless to me my belief.

Esther de Waal: The Celtic Vision.

ꝏꝏꝏꝏꝏꝏ

Deep peace of the Running Wave to you
Deep peace of the Flowing Air to you
Deep peace of the Quiet Earth to you
Deep peace of the Shining Stars to you
Deep peace of the Son of Peace to you

Traditional: A Celtic Blessing

ꝏꝏꝏꝏꝏꝏ

4

The Lament of the Earth

And let me speak to the yet unknowing world
How these things came about. So shall you hear
Of carnal, bloody, and unnatural acts;
Of accidental judgements, casual slaughters;
Of deaths put on by cunning and forced cause;
And, in the upshot, purposes mistook
Fall'n on the inventors' heads - all this can I
Truly deliver.

Hamlet: act 5, scene 2.

When an oake is being felled it gives a kind of shriekes and groanes, that may be heard a mile off, as if it were the genius of the oake lamenting.

Quoted by James Fraser: The Golden Bough.

ꝏꝏꝏꝏꝏꝏ

The forest is our livelihood. We have lived here before any of you outsiders came. We fished in clean rivers and hunted in the jungle. We made our sago meat and ate fruit of trees. Our life was not easy but we lived it in content. Now the logging companies turn rivers into muddy streams and the jungle into devastation. The fish cannot survive in dirty rivers and wild animals will not live in devastated forests. You took advantage of our trusting nature and cheated us into unfair deals. By your doing, you have taken away our livelihood and threaten our very lives. We want our ancestral land, the land we live on, back. We can use it in a wiser way. When you come to us, come as guests, with respect.

Declaration of the Penan people, Borneo.

ꝏꝏꝏꝏꝏꝏ

The Forest is our mother, our source of life, and in order to save it we will do everything we can until the end.

Chico Mendes, Rubber Tappers' Union Leader, assassinated 22nd December 1988. 'Link Up', No 38, Spring 1989.

ꝏꝏꝏꝏꝏꝏ

EARTHSONG

Come back, O Tigers! to the wood again,
And let it not be levelled with the plain;
For, without you, the axe will lay it low;
You, without it, for ever homeless go.

The Jataka.

ꝏꝏꝏꝏꝏꝏ

'Dawn, and the sun breaks through the piercing chill of night on the plain outside Korem, it lights up a biblical famine, now, in the twentieth century. This place, say workers here, is the closest thing to hell on earth'. There had been famine in Ethiopia since at least 1983, but it was this BBC television broadcast, in October 1984, which is generally credited with having broken through the veil of ignorance...

Famine, as a word, carries with it the implication that the user means to do something about it: bring help; criticise others for not doing enough; contribute to a charity collection; but certainly in some way to act. It is an acknowledgement that fellow human beings have reached the stage of utter despair where we must help.

Report for the Independent Commission on International Humanitarian Issues: Famine, a Man-Made Disaster?

ꝏꝏꝏꝏꝏꝏ

Born of earth
this brittle child of clay
baked by the sun kiln;
a thin figure rolled in mud,
fired in blistering heat,
this earth child, son of
rainless desert,
dust-child, shell spattered.

Only in his eyes
is the soil moist
and here it is stolen
by flies that crawl
like thieves
across the cracked chasm
of lips that bleed air.

Feed him rain;
Let his parchment-thin body
soak up liquid, breathe water.

Soften the cracked clay.

Siobhan Aiton (age 15): Earth Child.

ꝏꝏꝏꝏꝏꝏ

Watching television
In your desirable
Detached house
What do you see?
A detached tent.
That must be desirable -
The place to be;
A thousand moved in yesterday.
With an *en suite* desert
And a good chance of a sun tan,
This unusual property
Is conveniently situated
For the next relief lorry.
Running water - occasionally -
Plus excellent opportunities
For catching dysentry.
Viewing by appointment
On world TV.

Danny Conners (age 14): Residences.

The fish are all sick, the great whales dead,
the villages stranded in stone on the coast,
ornamental, like pearls on the fringe of a coat.
Sea men, who knew what the ocean did
turned their low houses away from the surf.
But new men, who came to be rural and safe,
add big glass views and begonia beds.

Water keeps to itself.
White lip after lip
curls to a close on the littered beach.
Something is sicker and blacker than fish.
And closing its grip, closing its grip.

Anne Stevenson: Selected Poems 1956-1986.

Pollution doesn't swim, fly, run, jump, scuttle or scamper.
It glides along with its jet black gown.
Acid rain killing forests and trees.
Rubbish blowing about in the breeze,
Nowhere for animals to sleep at night.
I hope the land will be all right.
It seems to me we live in danger.
Pollution is a horrible stranger.
Pollution is coming in his jet black gown.

Sarah Butcher (age 10): Pollution.

EARTHSONG

The disaster at Chernobyl touched a raw nerve in horrified onlookers, a sense that something was badly wrong in the world.

Many thoughtful people saw Chernobyl as a symbol of a world gone awry - a world in which technology was out of control. The list of disasters was a long one: the catastrophe of Bophal, the ruin of Times Beach, Missouri through dioxin pollution, the tragedy of Japan's mercury poisoned children, the wastage of Vietnam by Agent Orange, the devastation of Kyshtym, the horrifying spectacle of the explosion of Challenger, the destruction of the Black Forest by acid rain... a roll that could go on for pages.

Now, with Chernobyl there was a real demonstration of the dangers nuclear plants could pose.

Henry Hamman and Stuart Parrot: Mayday at Chernobyl.

ꝏꝏꝏꝏꝏ

Epitaph for Portavadie: an oil platform construction site on a remote part of the west coast of Scotland, developed at a cost of £14 million, and then never used.

I am here in name,
But my soul has fled,
I am writ in fame,
But I am dead;
Torn and battered,
Wrecked in style,
All for the sake of the genie,
Oil.
A cult of illusion,
The philosopher's stone,
The alchemy of oil
Is the new world's groan.
Technical experts to and fro,
And all around the pathogen grows.
Datelines, programmes, surveys arrange me.
(The heart doth not grieve what the eye does not see.)
For I am the victim of man's senseless power,
Blind to the truth of the jewel in the flower:
For what doth it profit a man to control
The whole of the world if he loses his soul?

S. Piper.

ꝏꝏꝏꝏꝏꝏ

When I see a green tree crying
and hear a mute fish dying.
Move me from selfishness to sharing
to watching and caring.

When I feel a neighbour sighing
and know that I am life denying.
Move me from selfishness to sharing
to loving and caring.

When I smell sick sky, sick sea, sick earth,
sick all
and taste living water dying.
Move me from selfishness to sharing
to healing and caring.

Erna Colebrook: Lament of a Consumerist.

Leader: In most aboriginal cultures of the Americas, the earth is called "Mother", as she is the source of blessings - food, clothing, shelter, medicines, beauty... God, the Creator and source of life, is called Great Spirit. Mother Earth speaks:

Voice: Listen, my children. The spirit who moved over the dry land is not pleased. I am thirsty. Are you listening?

All: We are listening, Mother Earth. Speak.

Voice: The spirit who filled the waters is not pleased. I choke with debris and pollution. Are you listening?

All: We are listening, Mother Earth. Speak.

Voice: The spirit who brought beauty to the earth is not pleased. I grow uglier everyday with misuse. Are you listening?

All: We are listening, Mother Earth. Speak.

Voice: The Spirit who brought all the creatures of this earth is not pleased. My creatures are being destroyed. Are you listening?

All: We are listening, Mother Earth. Speak.

Voice: The Spirit who gave humans life, and a path to walk together is not pleased. You are losing your humanity and your footsteps stray from the path, led by injustice. Are you listening?

All: We are listening, Mother Earth.
We are listening.

Leader: O God, you created the earth in goodness and in beauty. Forgive all that we have done to harm the earth.

EARTHSONG

All: God, have mercy.

Leader: O God, you have filled the earth with food for our sustenance. Forgive us for not sharing the gifts of the earth.

All: Christ, have mercy.

Leader: You have created us, O God, of one blood throughout the earth. Forgive us for not living as sisters and brothers should.

All: God, have mercy

Sister Rosita Shiosee: JPIC Resource Pack.

No one saw the first flash of the atomic fire itself. It was only possible to see its dazzling white reflection in the sky and on the hills...

People were transfixed with fright at the power of the explosion. Oppenheimer was clinging to one of the uprights in the control room. A passage from the *Bhagavad Gita*, the sacred epic of the Hindus, flashed into his mind.

If the radiance of a thousand suns
were to burst into the sky
that would be like
the splendour of the Mighty One.

Yet, when the sinister and gigantic cloud rose up in the far distance over Point Zero, he was reminded of another line from the same source:

I am become death, the shatterer of worlds.

Sri Krishna, the Exalted One, lord of the fate of mortals, had uttered the phrase. But Robert Oppenheimer was only a man.

Robert Jungk: Brighter than a Thousand Suns.

The birds were the things we could see all the time. They were superb specimens of life... really quite exquisite... phenomenal creatures. Albatrosses will fly for days, skimming a few inches above the surface of the water. These birds have tremendously long wings and tails... You don't see what these birds are about from their design, they are just beautiful creatures. Watching them is a wonder. That is what I didn't expect...

We were standing around waiting for this bomb to go off, which we were told was a very small one, so no one was particularly upset. Even though I'd never seen one, I figured, well, these guys know what is going to happen. They know what the dangers are and we've been adequately briefed and we all have our radiation meters on... no worry...

Anyway, we were standing around, and the countdown comes in over the radio. And we know roughly where the designated ground zero would be and about how high.

And suddenly I could see all these birds, I could see the birds I had been watching for days before. They were now suddenly visible through the opaque visor of my helmet. And they were smoking. Their feathers were on fire. And they were doing cartwheels. And the light persisted for some time. It was instantaneously bright but it wasn't instantaneous, because it stayed and it changed its composition slightly. Several seconds, it seemed like, long enough for me to see the birds crash into the water. They were sizzling, smoking. They weren't vapourised, it's just that they were absorbing such intense radiation that they were being consumed by the heat. Their feathers were on fire. They were blinded. And so far there had been no shock, none of the blast damage we talk about when we discuss the effects of nuclear weapons. Instead there were just those smoking, twisting hideously contorted birds crashing into things. And then I could see vapor rising from the inner lagoon as the surface of the water heated by this intense flash.

US Atom Test Observer, Christmas Island: quoted by Robert Scheer: With Enough Shovels.

ꝏꝏꝏꝏꝏꝏ

Solitudinem faciunt pacem appelant.
They make a desolation and call it peace.

Tacitus: Agricola.

ꝏꝏꝏꝏꝏꝏ

Oh, where have you been, my blue-eyed son?
Oh, where have you been, my darling young one?
I've stumbled on the side of twelve misty mountains,
I've walked and I've crawled on six crooked highways,
I've stepped in the middle of seven sad forests,
I've been out in front of a dozen dead oceans,
I've been ten thousand miles in the mouth of a graveyard,
And it's a hard, and it's a hard, it's a hard, and it's a hard,
And it's a hard rain's a-gonna fall.

Bob Dylan, Writings and Drawings.

ꝏꝏꝏꝏꝏꝏ

This is the *Fahrplananordnung 587*, which is typical for special trains. The number of the order goes to show you how many of them there were...

And here we see that starting out in one ghetto, which obviously is being emptied, the train leaves for Treblinka. It leaves on the thirtieth of September, 1942, eighteen minutes after four o'clock - by the schedule at least - and arrives there at eleven twenty-four on the next morning. This is also a very long train, which may be the reason it is so slow. It's a 50G - *fünfzig Güterwagen* - fifty freight cars filled with people. That's an exceptionally heavy transport. Now once the train has unloaded at Treblinka - and you notice there are two numbers here: 11:24, that's in the morning, and 15:59, which is to say almost four o'clock in the afternoon - in that interval of time the train has to be unloaded, cleaned and turned around. And you see here the same numbers appear as the *Leerzug*, the now empty train, goes to another place. And it leaves at four o'clock in the afternoon and goes now to that other place which is yet another small town where it picks up victims. And there you are at three o'clock in the morning... Then it goes back to Treblinka and this is again a long trip; and it now goes back to yet another place - the same situation, the same trip. And then yet another. Goes to Treblinka and then arrives in Czestochowa the twenty-ninth of September and then the cycle is complete... If you count up the number of full trains - PKRs - there's one - there's one here, that's two, that's three, that's four - we may be talking about ten thousand dead Jews on this one *Fahrplananordnung* here...

But why is this document so fascinating?

Well you see, when I hold a document in my hand, particularly if it's an original document, then I hold something which is actually something that the original bureaucrat held in his hand... The *Reichsbahn* was ready to ship, in principal, any cargo in return for payment and therefore the basic key, the price controlled key, was that Jews were going to be shipped to Treblinka, were going to be shipped to Auschwitz, Sobibor or any other destination so long as the railroads were going to be paid by the track kilometre, so many *pfennigs* per mile. The basic rate was the same throughout the war, with children under ten going for half fare, and children under four going free. Payment had to be made for only one way.

Excuse me, the children going to the extermination camps, the children under four?

Went free, their transport was free.

Roul Hilberg: quoted in Claude Lanzman: SHOAH.

ꝏꝏꝏꝏꝏꝏ

What greater pain could mortals have than this:
To see their children dead before their eyes

Euripides: Suppliant Women.

Turning and turning in the widening gyre
The falcon cannot hear the falconer;
Things fall apart; the centre cannot hold;
Mere anarchy is loosed upon the world,
The blood-dimmed tide is loosed, and everywhere
The ceremony of innocence is drowned;
The best lack all conviction, while the worst
Are full of passionate intensity.

Surely some revelation is at hand;
Surely the Second Coming is at hand.
The Second Coming! Hardly are those words out
When a vast image out of *Spiritus Mundi*
Troubles my sight: somewhere in sands of the desert
A shape with lion body and the head of a man,
A gaze blank and pityless as the sun,
Is moving its slow thighs, while all about it
Reel shadows of the indignant desert birds.
The darkness drops again; but now I know
That twenty centuries of stony sleep
Were vexed to nightmare by a rocking cradle,
And what rough beast, its hour come round at last,
Slouches towards Bethlehem to be born?

W. B. Yeats: The Second Coming.

How many roads must a man walk down
Before you call him a man?
Yes, 'n' how many seas must a white dove sail
Before she sleeps in the sand?
Yes, 'n' how many times must the cannon balls fly
Before they're forever banned?
The answer, my friend is blowin' in the wind,
The answer is blowin' in the wind.

How many times must a man look up
Before he can see the sky?
Yes, 'n' how many ears must one man have
Before he can hear people cry?
Yes, 'n' how many deaths will it take till he knows
That too many people have died?
The answer, my friend is blowin' in the wind,
The answer is blowin' in the wind.

How many years can a mountain exist
Before it's washed to the sea?
Yes, 'n' how many years can some people exist
Before they're allowed to be free?
Yes, 'n' how many times can a man turn his head,
Pretending he just doesn't see?
The answer, my friend is blowin' in the wind,
The answer is blowin' in the wind.

Bob Dylan: Writings and Drawings.

EARTHSONG

Listen now. Be still and hear
For creation takes up its Maker's call.
All creation draws near to God, seeks refuge from the tightening grip of winter, the winter our destruction has wrought; seeks light and warmth to revive that which we have darkened and chilled by our abuse of God's creation.

Listen to the Voices of Creation, the Advent of nature.

Air: Lord, I the Air come. Breath of life,
Wind that moves over the face of the deep
Bearing rain, I come.

Now the breath of life blows death.
As I pass over the land the broken soil follows me:
a billowing shroud of dust.

When the rain falls, forests and lakes die.

I come, my Lord.
But what have your people made of me
but a shadow, a dark acidic shadow,
of my God-given glory.
Breathe on your people, breath of God.

Voice: Hear the cry of our brother Air and bring light and life to the winter of our despair.

All: Breathe on your people, breath of God.

The Waters: We the Waters come, O Lord, flowing to meet you,
as we have flowed through time,
sustaining the life of all creation.

We come, O Lord, from our rivers and lakes,
our seas and oceans.

We come, O Lord, with our dead upon our waves.
Our living struggle against creeping filth
and our mighty creatures flee
before the fury of your people.

Can we ever recapture the purity of your will
in the brightness of our waters?
Stir up your people, O Lord,
to let the waters flow with life everlasting.

Voice: Hear the cry of our sister water and let light and life dispel the winter of our despair.

All: Stir up your people, O Lord.

The Land: Mountain and valley, hill and plain,
we the Land turn to you our Lord,
Ground of our ground.

Upon us you set your world,
from us called forth life in many forms.

THE LAMENT OF THE EARTH

In our richness you set the forests
On our fields you sowed the seed of life.

Gone are the forests, worn is the earth.
Silent in their graves lie the riches of your creation.

Gouged out are our mountains,
gone are the curves of our valley.
We who would bear your creation seek re-creation.
Plant in your people a love and respect for your Land.

Voice: Hear the cry of our Mother Earth and let light and life dispel the winter of our despair.

All: Plant in your people a love and respect for your land.

Creatures: From the water, air and land
we the creatures came forth at your command.

From dust you raised us and in us planted your life.

Through the ways of Time
you brought us to Be.

Now we come, called forth again.
Yet many can no longer come.
Gone, gone for ever.

And we, we who come.
Can we know our children's
children will know this world?

So much has gone. What remains is so frail.
Free your people from their ignorance and selfishness.

Voice: Hear the cry of those who dwell in air and sea and land and let your life and light dispel the winter of our despair.

All: Free your people from their ignorance and selfishness.

Humanity: We, your people, come.
We, who crucify this world, stripping bare its soil,
crowning it with a wreath of broken trees.
Its air breathes painfully,
its waters weep for the folly that poisons them,
its creatures bleed.
We have eaten and drunk of life's body.

Heirs of all, we have sold our world.
Thirty pieces of silver is our price.
Loudly declaring our love, we have denied our Lord.

We are Judas, we are Peter.
We are the cross of all creation.

All: Lord, in your advent, help us resurrect the glory of your creation for our children and our children's children.

Martin Palmer & Anne Nash: Advent and Ecology.

EARTHSONG

When we do not let our tears flow in time, there can be no thoughts of peace but only pure horror.

Tears are a mercy. They are the beginning of the solace which we will find when we summon up the courage to look the horrors in the face. As long as we push away these horrors we only shrivel up, so that our seemingly intelligent and resolute actions only bring forth the disasters which in our minds they should have prevented. With our tears we give up all hope of being in control of our own fate. The living hope - of that which is not in our power - is born again and with it the freedom to true action. Only then do we see the breaking of a new day.

Carl Friedrich von Weizsäcker: Die Zeit Drängt. Translation by Erna Colebrook.

Death has to be waiting at the end of the ride before you truly see the earth, and feel your heart, and love the world.

Jean Anouilh: The Lark.

5

New Things are struggling to their Birth

From the beginning till now the entire creation, as we know, has been groaning in one great act of giving birth; and not only creation, but all of us who possess the first-fruits of the Spirit, we too groan inwardly as we wait for our bodies to be set free.

Romans: 8,22-23: Jerusalem Bible.

A wind has blown across the world
And tremors shake its frame;
New things are struggling to their birth
And naught shall be the same.
The earth is weary of its past,
Of folly, hate and fear;
Beyond a dark and stormy sky
The dawn of God is near.

F. C. Happold: The Journey Inwards.

Who stands at my door in the storm and rain
On the threshold of being?
One who waits till you call him in
From the empty night.

Are you a stranger, out in the storm,
Or has my enemy found me out
On the edge of being?

I am no stranger who stands at the door
Nor enemy come in the secret night,
I am your child, in darkness and fear
On the verge of being.

Go back, my child, to the rain and storm,
For in this house there is sorrow and pain
In the lonely night.

I will not go back for sorrow and pain,
For my true love weeps within
And waits for my coming.

EARTHSONG

Go back, my babe, to the vacant night
For in this house dwell sin and hate
On the verge of being.

I will not go back for hate or sin,
I will not go back for sorrow and pain,
For my true love mourns within
On the threshold of night.

Kathleen Raine.

I cry
For the lichens and the mosses that grow on the stone,
The timeless granite boulders.

I cry
For the grasses and flowers that colour the
Wind-swept landscape.

I cry
For the beauty of the natural world, the perfect
Balance, the perfect poem.

I cry
For all the unborn generations.

I cry
For my long lost innocence.

I cry
With my fear.

My tears fall on the stones, the soil,
Make my tears give you life.
Make my despair give you hope.
Make my fear turn to trust.
Make my deeds be enough.

Helen Colebrook: A walk on the Moor.

I see his blood upon the rose,
And in the stars the glory of his eyes,
His body gleams amid eternal snows,
His tears fall from the skies.

I see his face in every flower;
The thunder and singing of the birds
Are but his voice - and carven by his power;
Rocks are his written words.

All pathways by his feet are worn,
His strong heart stirs the ever-beating sea,
His crown of thorns is twined of every thorn,
His cross is every tree.

Joseph Mary Plunkett.

Be assured, I am with you always, to the end of time.

Matthew: 28, 20. New English Bible.

I believe,
no pain is lost.
No tear unmarked,
no cry of anguish
dies unheard,
lost in the hail of gunfire
or blanked out by the padded cell.
I believe that pain
and prayer
are somehow saved,
processed,
stored,
used in the Divine Economy.
The blood
shed in Salvador
will irrigate the heart
of some financier
a million miles away.
The terror,
pain,
despair,
swamped
by lava, flood or earthquake
will be caught up
like mist and fall again,
a gentle rain
on arid hearts
or souls despairing
in the back streets
of Brooklyn.

Sheila Cassidy: Sharing the Darkness.

It's not an ordinary time,
Not an ordinary time at all.
It's a time for heroes
Those who can face facts
Though they sear like a red-hot iron
From the heart of a Pittsburgh furnace.
Come close you who dare, but unless there are
some who do come close
What hope, oh world? What hope, ye lands and
seas and inhabitors thereof?
All will disintegrate,

EARTHSONG

All will be gone.
"Business as usual", is the cry of most,
As they draw their blinkers more tightly
Around their eyes,
Shielding themselves as best they may
From the heat of the flame
Clinging desperately to whatever remains
Of the familiar world
Of yesteryear
Of yesterday.
Others see the doom that is at hand -
You don't really need to be a detective -
But they pour out their life force in protest
And protest is a deceitful god
That sucks dry the blood of the people
And at the end of the day
Is silent
And helpless
As Baal was silent and helpless.
The infamy has already been wrought
The damage has already been done
The evils already are here
Hunger and inflation and plutonium and a
thousand more
Spawn of human arrogance and selfishness and
fear...
The world as we know it cannot survive them
And will not survive them.

All this the hero sees
But he sees something else also
A way
A way through the inferno
A way through the desert
A way through famine and pestilence, war and
earthquakes
A hero's way
Not a way of survival
But a way of life
A way of strength and effectiveness
A way of assurance
A way of calm
Born of his unwavering love for the One who still
Even in these turbulent times
Especially in these turbulent times
Is Lord of Heaven and Earth.

The hero goes quietly to work
Needing no chariot
No spear
No audience
No praise
No reward.
His arena is the circumstance where he is

And into that arena he pours himself
And his own indomitable spirit
The building block of a new order
A true order
A spiritual order.
The old world crumbles under the pressure of
    what he brings
And out of the confusion and darkness
A new world appears
Filled with magic and light.

Chris Foster: A Time for Heroes.

ꝏꝏꝏꝏꝏꝏ

The human heart can go to the lengths of God.
Dark and cold we may be, but this is no winter now.
The frozen misery of centuries breaks, cracks, begins to move;
The thunder is the thunder of the floes,
The thaw, the flood, the upstart spring.
Thank God our time is now when wrong comes up to face us everywhere,
Never to leave till we take the longest stride of soul men ever took.
Affairs are now soul size.
The enterprise is exploration into God.

Christopher Fry: A Sleep of Prisoners.

ꝏꝏꝏꝏꝏꝏ

O, tell us, poet, what do you do? - I praise.
But those dark, deadly, devastating ways,
how do you bear them, suffer them? - I praise.
And then the Nameless, beyond guess or gaze,
how can you call it, conjure it? - I praise.
And whence your right in every kind of maze,
in every mask, to remain true? - I praise.
And that the mildest and the wildest ways
know you like star and storm? - Because I praise.

Rainer Maria Rilke.

ꝏꝏꝏꝏꝏꝏ

EARTHSONG

In the midst of hunger and war
We celebrate the promise of plenty and peace.
In the midst of oppression and tyranny
We celebrate the promise of service and freedom.
In the midst of doubt and despair
We celebrate the promise of faith and hope.
In the midst of fear and betrayal
We celebrate the promise of joy and happiness.
In the midst of hatred and death
We celebrate the promise of love and life.
In the midst of sin and decay
We celebrate the promise of salvation and renewal.
In the midst of death on every side
We celebrate the promise of the living Christ.

World Council of Churches: Worship book of the 7th Assembly.

We are the bridge where the worlds meet
We are the spirit made manifest
Its essence the subtle form we are standing in
Reflecting the visible meaning of anything
In us, as us, and through us as it is
We are everything we have forgotten
we are here to remember and re-begin
People of God - we *are* God
When I say, my friend, I believe in you
Seeing your face in its feeling fineness
Feeling that light you have brought
Uniquely to life in each cell of you
Our being. freed from its chains, its dying
Is passionate realisation - we have come
To live what is ours, to bring it through
And rise like the ground within us
Up through our hearts, heads, hands and eyes
This is a generation to end all generations
This is the place and this is the time
And when I know what we can be, I am alive
I can see, we are the poem, we are its prophecy

WE ARE THE RAINBOW
SCORED ACROSS THE THUNDERCLOUD
WE ARE THE TREE OF LIVE
AND THE DESERT AROUND
WE ARE THE CAUSE

WE ARE THE SEED AND THE SEA
WE ARE THE FUTURE
WE ALWAYS HAVE BEEN
Say it out loud
THIS IS OUR BIRTH AND OUR BREAKING
THIS IS THE CHOICE WE ARE MAKING

Jay Ramsay: New Age.

In a dark time, the eye begins to see.

Theodore Roethke.

6

Finding our Way

There be three things which are too wonderful for me,
yea, four which I know not:
the way of an eagle in the air,
the way of a serpent upon a rock,
the way of a ship on the midst of the sea,
and the way of a man with a maid.

Proverbs: 30, 18–19: Revised Version.

Then from the heart of the tempest God gave Job his answer. He said:

Where were you when I laid the earth's foundations?
 Tell me, since you are so well-informed.
Who decided the dimensions of it, do you know?
 Or who stretched the measuring line across it?
What supports its pillars at their bases?
 Who laid its cornerstone?
Who pent up the sea behind closed doors
 when it leapt tumultuous out of the womb,
when I wrapped it in a robe of mist
 and made black clouds its swaddling bands;
when I marked the bounds it was not to cross
 and made it fast with a bolted door?
Come thus far, I said, and no farther:
 here your proud waves shall break.

Can you fasten the harness of the Pleiades,
 or untie Orion's bands?
Can you guide the morning star season by season
 and show the Bear and its cubs which way to go?
Have you grasped the celestial laws?
 Could you make their writ run on the earth?
Can you make your voice carry as far as the clouds
 and make the pent up waters do your bidding?
Will lightning flashes come at your command
 and answer 'Here we are'?
Whose skill details every cloud
 and tilts the flasks of heaven
until the soil cakes into a solid mass
 and clods of earth cohere together?

EARTHSONG

Do you find a prey for the lioness
 and satisfy the hunger of her whelps
when they crouch in their dens
 and lurk in their lairs?
Who makes provision for the raven
 when his squabs cry out to God
and crane their necks in hunger?

Who gave the wild donkey his freedom,
 and untied the rope from his proud neck?
I have given him the desert as a home,
 and the salt plains as his own habitat.
He scorns the turmoil of the town:
 there are no shouts from a driver for him to listen for.
The mountains are the pastures that he ranges
 in quest of any type of green blade or leaf.

Does the hawk take flight on your advice
 when he spreads his wings to travel south?
Does the eagle soar at your command
 to make her eyrie in the heights?

Job: 38-39 (excerpts), the Jerusalem Bible.

Today God's words might have a similar thunderous challenge.

How is it since you are so clever and can reach the moon, that you cannot overcome the difficulties that prevent you from feeding the hungry who are so near to you?

How is it, since you claim to understand the workings of nature, that you cannot harness the wind, the waves and the sun for your power but have to resort to methods which pollute and poison the earth?

How is it, since you claim to understand the workings of human nature, that you cannot devise ways to live in peace except by possessing the threat of mutual extinction?

How is it, since you claim to understand so much about man's economic life, that you cannot live in a way so that mankind can work to glorify his Creator and enjoy the fruits and blessings of the earth?

How is it, since you claim to know so much about the workings of nature, that you are overburdening its inbuilt systems for cleansing and renewal so that many forms of life are threatened and natural mechanisms are breaking down?

How is it that since you replaced the law of God with your own wisdom, you have turned the world into a place where people are driven by fear and greed, where the first invitation of God to man - to go and multiply - has become the curse on which the evils of the world are blamed?

Barbara Wood: Our World God's World.

We stand at a crossroads. In the past the pursuit of 'progress' in the industrialised West was founded on four dominant beliefs: that people dominate the earth, that they are masters of their destiny, that the world is vast and unlimited, and that history is the process of advancement, with every problem solvable. But we must now call into question these four basic beliefs. Instead, the essential basis for sustainable development must be concern for the world's environment. We need individual participation at all levels in the care of the planet and, based on this deeper and wider perception of the basis of life and human activity, we need profound changes in economic and social attitiudes. If the planet is to be saved, this is a battle we are all called to fight.

Gro Harlem Brundtland: quoted in Andre Singer: Battle for the Planet.

∞∞∞∞∞∞∞∞

This year the earth spoke, like God warning Noah of the deluge. Its message was loud and clear, and suddenly people began to listen, to ponder what portents the message held. In the U.S., a three month drought baked the soil from California to Georgia, reducing the country's grain harvest by 31%... Pollution closed beaches on the Mediterranean, the North Sea and the English Channel. Killer hurricanes ripped through the Caribbean and floods devastated Bangladesh, reminders of nature's raw power. In Soviet Armenia a monstrous earthquake killed some 25,000 people. That too was a natural disaster, but the high casualty count, owing largely to the construction of cheap high-rise apartment blocks over a well-known fault area, illustrated the carelessness that has become humanity's habit in dealing with nature... This year's bout of freakish weather and environmental horror stories seemed to act as a powerful catalyst for worldwide public opinion. Everybody suddenly sensed that the gyrating globe, this precious repository of all the life that we know was in danger.

Thomas Sancton: Time International, January 1989.

∞∞∞∞∞∞∞∞

We know that everything is evolving. The future of that evolution on our planet is now in our hands. We have the power to destroy or enhance the life process on Earth. Which path we choose to take is our supreme moral decision.

That brings us to the question of what precisely should steer our decisions. The universal unfolding gives us a clear answer. For 3½ billion years life, in myriad forms, has been engaged in a struggle to establish, expand and enhance its manifestation on Earth. This process started with a mass of undifferentiated microscopic cells floating in the primeval sea. Now we have highly complex creatures, cities, computers, space travel. Our role is to carry that process foward in such a way as to enhance the quality of life on the planet and ensure its future development.

James Hemming, Lords of the Unknown Future. The Guardian, 30 January, 1989.

In the Creed we affirm that we believe in God the Creator of Heaven and Earth. But what do we mean by this? Often the way we speak about God as Creator makes him sound like an absentee landlord. Visions of Blake's God with the dividers come to mind, but we lack any real sense of God as both Creator and sustainer...

In looking at God the Creator, what are we to make of the purpose of the rest of creation? Millions of years have passed in the life of the planet. Evolution and geological forces of the earth have created multitudes of life and species, mountains and valleys which no human being ever saw. Can we really believe that all existence was made solely for us? If we do not believe this, then what does this tell us about the value of all life to God, its source and its sustainer?

There is a Jewish quotation which says that no man should be allowed to read the first two chapters of Genesis alone for there are so many unanswered questions and so many unanswerable questions therein they would drive a man insane. We do well to remember this as we grapple with these vast issues. There may be no clear answers but what is certain is that unless we make ourselves think hard we will continue to use models of God the Creator which simply are inadequate both to the Biblical heritage and to the task of saving life on earth.

World Wildlife Fund: Creation and Harvest.

If one were to do Christian theology from the holistic perspective, it is evident that some significant changes from traditional models and concepts would be necessary for expressing the relationships between God and the world and between ourselves and the world. Language that supports hierarchical, dualistic, external, unchanging, atomistic, anthropocentric, and deterministic ways of understanding these relationships is not appropriate *for our time*, whatever its appropriateness might have been for other times. It would appear that the appropriate language for our time, in the sense of being true to the paradigm of reality in which we actually live, would support ways of understanding the God-world and human-world relationships as open, caring, inclusive, interdependent, changing, mutual, and creative.

Needless to say, I am not proposing that the only criterion for theology is its fit with the reigning understanding of reality. But for theology to do *less* than fit our present understanding—for it to accept basic assumptions about reality from a very different time—seems blatantly wrongheaded.

Sallie McFague: Models of God.

∞∞∞∞∞∞∞∞

The traditional Judeo-Christian doctrine of creation... evokes such terms as *'viceregent', 'steward', 'trustee'* or *'manager'* to represent the human role in nature. However, these terms still introduce a nuance of 'domination' into the biblical concept of 'dominion' and, in modern English, do not adequately convey the 'caring' component inherent in the Biblical understanding... [The] proper responses of man to nature may also be conceived as that of *priest of creation*, as a result of whose activity the sacrament of creation is reverenced; and who, because he alone is conscious of God, himself and nature, can mediate between insentient nature and God - for a priest is characterised by activity directed towards God on behalf of others.

Arthur Peacocke: God and the New Biology.

∞∞∞∞∞∞∞∞

Life is a phenomenon that exists on a planetary scale... By taking the species and their physical environment together as a single system, we can build ecological models that provide a justification for diversity.

We have at last a reason for our instinctive anger over the heedless deletion of species; an answer to those who say it is mere sentimentality. No longer do we have to justify the existence of the humid tropical forest on the feeble grounds that they might carry plants with drugs that could cure human disease... Through their capacity to evaporate vast volumes of water from the surface of their leaves, trees serve to keep the planet cool with a sunshade of white reflecting clouds. Their replacement by cropland could precipitate a disaster of global scale.

Geophysical systems grow from the activity of individual organisms. When the growth of the organism benefits the environment as well as the organism itself, then its spread will be assisted. The reverse is also true: any species that adversely affects the environment is doomed, but life goes on.

EARTHSONG

Does this apply to humans now? Are we doomed by our destruction of the natural world, by changing the previous comfortable state of the Earth to one almost certainly unfavourable for us, but comfortable to the new biosphere of our successors?

James Lovelock: Gaia: the World as a Living Organism. New Scientist, 18 December 1986.

Grandfather
Look at our brokenness,
we know that in all creation
only the human family
has strayed away from the sacred way.
We know we are the ones
who are divided.
And we are the ones
who must come back together
to walk in the sacred way.
Grandfather, sacred one,
teach us love, compassion and honour
that we may heal the earth
and heal each other.

from the Ojibway nation of Canada: quoted in Barbara Wood, Our World God's World.

The fertility of soil, the diversity of species, clean water and air, equable climate - these are the real wealth of the planet, its capital resources. In a steady-state world, we would not deplete this capital by careless exploitation. We would guard and replenish it, living on the income generated by seasonal growth and the energy of the sun and earth, and by the recycling of used resources. The old economic imperative, defining "growth" as rising consumption and GNP, is discredited in such a system. But *real* growth is possible - the better we care for the capital base, the more efficiently conserve, recycle and renew the income, the greater the "flow" of resources. Even with abundant clean energy, however, there are finite limits to a sustainable income. One cannot deny poor countries the right to a better future; rather living standards in rich countries may have to fall. Both must seek to replace the ethics of materialism with a desire for a shared well-being.

Frank Barnaby (Ed): The Gaia Peace Atlas.

But the change of mind I am talking about involves not just a change in knowledge, but also a change of attitude toward our essential ignorance, a change in our bearing in the face of mystery. The principle of ecology, if we will take it to heart, should keep us aware that our lives depend upon other lives and upon processes and energies in an interlocked system that, though we can destroy it, we can neither fully understand nor fully control. And our great dangerousness is that, locked in our selfish and myopic economics, we have been willing to change or destroy far beyond our power to understand.

Wendell Berry: A Continuous Harmony.

Man has every right to be anxious about his fate so long as he feels himself to be lost and lonely in the midst of created things. But let him once discover that his fate is bound up with nature itself, and immediately, joyously, he will begin his forward march.

Pierre Teilhard de Chardin: Hymn of the Universe.

It is the nature of any organic pattern to be part of a larger one. And so a good solution in one pattern preserves the integrity of the pattern that contains it. A good agricultural solution, for example, would not pollute or erode a watershed. What is good for the water is good for the ground, what is good for the ground is good for plants, what is good for plants is good for animals, what is good for animals is good for people, what is good for people is good for the air, what is good for the air is good for the water. And vice versa.

Wendell Berry: The Gift of Good Land.

The art of living is based on rhythm, on give and take, ebb and flow, light and dark, life and death. By acceptance of all the aspects of life, good and bad, right and wrong, yours and mine, the static defensive life, which is what most people are cursed with, is converted into a dance, 'the dance of life'... The real function of the dance is metamorphosis...

Henry Miller: from the introduction to 'The Mind of the Druid' by Graham Howe.

EARTHSONG

The Lakota was a true lover of nature. He loved the earth and all things of the earth, the attachment growing with age. The old people came literally to love the soil and they sat and reclined on the ground with a feeling of being close to a mothering power. It was good for the skin to touch the earth and the old people liked to remove their moccasins and walk with bare feet on the sacred earth. Their tipis were built upon the earth and their altars were made of earth. The birds that flew in the air came to rest upon the earth and it was the final resting place of all things that lived and grew. The soil was soothing, strengthening, cleansing and healing.

That is why the old Indian still sits upon the earth instead of propping himself up and away from its life-giving forces. For him, to sit or lie upon the ground is to be able to think more deeply and to feel more keenly; he can see more clearly into the mysteries of life and come closer in kinship to other lives about him...

Kinship with all creatures of the earth, sky and water was a real and active principle. For the animal and bird world there existed a brotherly feeling that kept the Lakota safe among them and so close did some of the Lakota come to their feathered and furred friends that in true brotherhood they spoke a common tongue.

The old Lakota was wise. He knew that man's heart away from nature becomes hard; he knew that lack of respect for growing, living things soon led to lack of respect for humans too. So he kept his youth close to its softening influence.

Chief Luther Standing Bear: quoted in T C McLuhan: Touch the Earth.

∞∞∞∞∞∞∞

We can say today that man is far too clever to be able to survive without wisdom. No-one is really working for peace unless he is working primarily for the restoration of wisdom... The hope that the pursuit of goodness and virtue can be postponed until we we have attained universal prosperity and that by the single-minded pursuit of wealth, without bothering our heads about spiritual and moral questions, we could establish peace on earth, is an unrealistic, unscientific, and irrational hope. The exclusion of wisdom from economics, science, and technology was something we could perhaps get away with for a little while, as long as we were relatively unsuccessful; but now that we have become very successful, the problem of spiritual and moral truth moves into the central position...

The cultivation and expansion of needs is the antithesis of wisdom. It is also the antithesis of freedom and justice. Every increase of needs tends to increase one's dependence on outside forces over which one cannot have control, and therefore increases existential fear. Only by a reduction of needs can one promote a genuine reduction in those tensions which are the ultimate causes of strife and war.

E. F. Schumacher: Small is Beautiful.

'When someone is seeking', said Siddhartha, 'it happens quite easily that he only sees the thing that he is seeking; that he is unable to find anything, unable to absorb anything, because he is only thinking of the thing he is seeking, because he has a goal, because he is obsessed with his goal. Seeking means: to have a goal; but finding means: to be free, to be receptive, to have no goal. You, O worthy one, are perhaps indeed a seeker, for in striving towards your goal, you do not see many things that are under your nose'... 'Wisdom is not communicable. The wisdom which a wise man tries to communicate always sounds foolish'...

'Knowledge can be communicated, but not wisdom. One can find it, live it, be fortified by it, do wonders through it, but one cannot communicate and teach it...

Hermann Hesse: Siddarthar.

Yahweh created me when his purpose first unfolded,
before the oldest of his works.
From everlasting I was firmly set,
from the beginning, before earth came into being...
I was by his side, mistress of my craft,
delighting him day after day,
ever at play in his presence,
at play everywhere in his world,
delighting to be with the children of men.

Words spoken by a personification of Wisdom in Proverbs: 8, 22–23 & 30–31. Jerusalem Bible (altered).

If we enter a rainforest and allow our energies to merge with the energies that we find there, then the rainforest may be a place where our roots are able to penetrate through the soft soil into the reality of our billions of years of carbon journey through the universe. Various truths which heretofor had been merely 'scientific' become authentic, personal and, yes, spiritual. We may now penetrate to a truly deep ecology.

Much of the apathy and paralysis that prevents us from throwing our lives into Earth-defence and Earth-healing is a product of our shrunken sense of self. As long as we remain identified with the social fictions we have been conditioned to believe compose our 'self', it is indeed difficult to find the energy and resolve necessary for the successful defence of Nature. If we can allow our sense of self to deepen, however, then our actions can be seen to be 'self-defence', for the Nature that we defend is no other than our own.

Once we have experienced the fierce joy of life that attends extending our identity into 'external' Nature, boundless energy and enthusiasm are ours for the asking. Once we realise that the Nature in here and the Nature out there are one and the same, then we act with passion and wisdom to prevent the destruction of the Tree of Life on which we humans are but a tiny blossom.

John Seed: The Rainforest Information Centre, Australia.

ꝏꝏꝏꝏꝏꝏ

Caring for and cultivating the world God created, perfect though it is, is part of his plan for mankind and the means by which we reflect his glory.

This is the context in which we should put all our work. It should be a means by which we reflect God and glorify God. This is so both in the way we do our work and also in the ends we are trying to achieve in the work we do. Clearly work that ultimately - as a by-product or as its final product - destroys God's creation, is not going to be an activity that leads us to God or can reflect his glory... Our work is more than a means to obtaining the basic necessities of life; it is an involvement in the divine creative process; it is an act of prayer; it is a means by which we grow towards God; it is the means by which we grow towards and work out our relationship with others...

It is by emphasising only the material ends of our work to the exclusion of the spiritual and social aspects that we have neglected to see its relevance to our salvation.

Barbara Wood: Our world God's World.

ꝏꝏꝏꝏꝏꝏ

How can you love your neighbor if you dont know how to build or mend a fence, how to keep your filth out of his water supply and your poison out of his air; or if you do not produce anything and so have nothing to offer, or do not take care of yourself and so become a burden. How can you be a neighbor without applying principle - without bringing virtue to a practical issue? How will you practice virtue without skill?

The ability to be good is not the ability to do nothing. It is not negative or passive. It is the ability to do something well - to do good work for good reasons. In order to be good you must know how - and this knowing is vast, complex, humble and humbling; it is of the mind and of the hands.

Wendell Berry: The Gift of Good Land.

ꝏꝏꝏꝏꝏꝏ

Here is a test to find
whether your mission on earth is finished:
If you're alive,
it isn't.

Learning
is finding out what you already know.
Doing is demonstrating that you know it.
Teaching is reminding others
That they know as well as you.

You are all learners, doers, teachers.

Messiah's Handbook: Reminders for the Advanced Soul.

ꝏꝏꝏꝏꝏꝏ

We must do what we conceive to be the right thing and not bother our heads or burden our souls with whether we're going to be successful. Because if we don't do the right thing, we'll be doing the wrong thing, and we'll just be part of the disease and not part of the cure.

E F Schumacher.

ꝏꝏꝏꝏꝏꝏ

Let there be many windows in your soul,
That all the glory of the universe
May beautify it. Not the narrow pane
Of one poor creed can catch the radiant ways
That shine from countless sources. Tear away
The blinds of superstition; let the light
Pour through fair windows, broad as truth itself
And high as heaven... Tune your ear
To all the wordless music of the stars
And to the voice of nature, and your heart
Shall turn to goodness as the plant
Turns to the sun. A thousand unseen hands
Reach down to help you to their peace-crowned heights,
And all the forces of the firmament
Shall fortify your strength. Be not afraid
To thrust aside half-truths and grasp the whole.

Ralph Waldo Trine: In tune with the Infinite.

ꝏꝏꝏꝏꝏꝏ

EARTHSONG

This is the bread;
The most important thing to do with it is eat it.
Who baked the loaf, and how, who sowed the seed,
is relevant, but all of that can wait.

And how the universe, of which this loaf is a fantastic part,
first came to be is worth a thought,
Which you will never have, unless you have to eat;

How anything can ever be at all is something to wonder at;
for none can live by bread alone
But show me any who can get along without it.

This is where all faith and wonder start:
By eating and drinking what is offered,
The Body and the Blood
The sacrament you must take to stay alive.

Sydney Carter (altered)

And he gave it for his opinion, that whoever could make two ears of corn or two blades of grass to grow upon a spot of ground where only one grew before, would deserve better of mankind, and do more essential service to his country than the whole race of politicians put together.

Jonathan Swift: Gulliver's Travels.

The Green Revolution - the utilization of new seed varieties, combined with fertilizers and pesticides - was designed to be a technological solution to the world's food problems...

The principal, or intended, effect of the Green Revolution - increased food production - seems to have been achieved. Unfortunately the social side-effects have not been entirely beneficial in most regions where the new seed varieties have been introduced...

Where conditions of economic inequality already exist, the Green Revolution tends to cause widening inequality. Large farmers generally adopt the new methods first. They have the capital to do so and can afford to take the risk... On large farms, simple economic considerations lead almost inevitably to the use of labour-displacing machinery and to the purchase of more land. The ultimate effects of this socio-economic positive feedback loop are agricultural unemployment, increased migration to the city, and perhaps even increased malnutrition, since the poor and unemployed do not have the means to buy the newly produced food.

Donella Meadows, et al: The Limits to Growth.

In our days everything seems pregnant with its contrary. Machinery gifted with the wonderful power of shortening and fructifying human labour, we behold starving and overworking it. The new-fangled sources of wealth, by some strange weird spell are turned into sources of want.

Mikhail Gorbachev: quoted in Kate Soper: END Journal, 31, December-January 1987/88.

Human institutions which grow up in response to various needs, necessities, insights, possibilities and even revelations in order to promote human betterment regularly become sources of human distortion, dis-service and even potential destruction.

David Jenkins: God, Politics and the Future.

Who could remain indifferent faced with the rapid deterioration of the natural environment which had stayed unchanged throughout the whole of human history? The increase in natural disasters caused by human activity and the demographic pressure on resources which are already limited make the environment an inescapable problem.

The problem of the environment cannot be separated from the problem of development. In order to provoke an awareness and take initiatives which are not founded upon anxiety, it is primarily important to provide full and scientific news information.

The UN could create an environmental observatory with antennae in every continent. This would permit an unbroken supervision and a definition of the limits of exploitation of natural resources, animals or plants, as well as regulations for the checking of industrial pollution.

Like the creation of the Food and Agricultural Organisation, the UN should create an International Air Agency and an International Water Agency. These organisations would pay particular attention to the threat of climatic changes caused by human activities.

Youth Suggestions for the UN, Letter from Taizé, February, 1989.

Further global progress is now possible only through a quest for universal consensus in the movement towards a new world order...

The international community has to learn to form and channel processes in such a way as to save civilization and to make the world a safer place for all of us...

What I am referring to is the kind of cooperation that could be called 'co-creativity' and 'co-development'.

The concept of development at another's expense is becoming obsolete. Today's realities make any genuine progress impossible if it disregards human and national rights and freedoms, or is detrimental to the environment...

Crucial changes and revolutionary transformations are sure to take place in this or that country and social structure. This has always been the case and always will be...

In the past, differences often acted as barriers; today they can develop into factors of rapprochment and mutual enrichment...

In thinking all this over, it becomes clear that we have to look for ways together to improve the international situation, to build a new world - that is, if we are going to take into consideration the lessons of the past, the realities of the present, and the objective logic of world development.

Mikhail Gorbachev, Address to the United Nations, December 1988.

And that disciple who was called Hafiz said unto him: "Master, tell us of the city of Orphalese, and of that land wherin you tarried those twelve years."

And Almustafa was silent, and he looked away toward the hills and toward the vast ether, and there was a battle in his silence.

Then he said: 'My friends and my road-fellows, pity the nation that is full of beliefs and empty of religion.

'Pity the nation that wears a cloth it does not weave, eats a bread it does not harvest, and drinks a wine that flows not from its own wine-press.

'Pity the nation that acclaims the bully as hero, and that deems the glittering conqueror bountiful.

'Pity a nation that despises a passion in its dream, yet submits in its awakening.

'Pity the nation that raises not its voice save when it walks in a funeral, boasts not except among its ruins, and will rebel not save when its neck is laid between the sword and the block.

'Pity the nation whose statesman is a fox, whose philosopher is a juggler, and whose art is the art of patching and mimicking.

'Pity the nation that welcomes its new ruler with trumpetings, and farewells him with hootings, only to welcome another with trumpetings again.

'Pity the nation whose sages are dumb with years and whose strong men are yet in the cradle.

'Pity the nation divided into fragments, each fragment deeming itself a nation.'

Kahlil Gibran: The Garden of the Prophet.

Plurality which is not reduced to unity is confusion; unity which does not depend on plurality is tyranny.

Blaise Pascal: Pensées.

Enjoy the earth gently
Enjoy the earth gently
For if the earth is spoiled
It cannot be repaired
Enjoy the earth gently

Yoruba poem, West Africa.

EARTHSONG

Almost everything you will do will be insignificant, but it is very important that you do it.

Mahatma Gandhi.

ꝏꝏꝏꝏꝏꝏ

This list of values and questions for discussion were composed by a diverse group of people who are working to build a new politics which has kinship with Green movements around the world...

1. ECOLOGICAL WISDOM - How can we operate human societies with the understanding that we are part of nature, not on top of it?

2. GRASSROOTS DEMOCRACY - How can we develop systems that allow and encourage us to control the decisions that affect our lives?

3. PERSONAL AND SOCIAL RESPONSIBILITY - How can we respond to human suffering in ways that promote dignity?

4. NONVIOLENCE - How can we as a society, develop effective alternatives to our current patterns of violence, at all levels, from the family and the street to nations and the world?

5. DECENTRALIZATION - How can we restore power and responsibility to individuals, institutions, communities and regions? How can we encourage the flourishing of regionally-based culture rather than a dominant mono-culture?

6. COMMUNITY BASED ECONOMICS - How can we redesign our work structures to encourage employee ownership and workplace democracy? How can we develop new economic activities and institutions that will allow us to use our new technologies in ways that are humane, freeing, ecological and accountable and responsive to communities?

7. POSTPATRIARCHAL VALUES - How can we replace the cultural ethics of dominance and control with more cooperative ways of interacting?

8. RESPECT FOR DIVERSITY - How can we honor cultural, ethnic, racial, sexual, religious and spiritual diversity within the context of responsibility toward all beings?

9. GLOBAL RESPONSIBILITY - How can we be of genuine assistance to grassroots groups in the Third World? What can we learn from them?

Charlene Spretnak: The Spiritual Dimension of Green Politics.

ꝏꝏꝏꝏꝏꝏ

Changing the structures of society is fundamentally a matter of politics. It requires a political strategy based on a clear social and political analysis. The Church has to address itself to these strategies and to the analysis upon which they are based. It is into this situation that the Church has to bring the gospel. Not as an alternative solution to our problems as if the gospel provided us with a non-political solution to political problems. There is no specifically Christian solution. There will be a Christian way of approaching the political solutions, a Christian spirit and motivation and attitude. But there is no way of bypassing politics and political strategies.

But we have still not pinpointed the fundamental problem. Why has 'Church Theology' not developed a social analysis? Why does it have an inadequate understanding of the need for political strategies? And why does it make a virtue of neutrality and sitting on the sidelines?

The answer must be sought in the *type of faith and spirituality* that has dominated Church life for centuries. As we all know, spirituality has tended to be an other-worldly affair that has very little, if anything at all, to do with the affairs of this world... Moreover, spirituality has been understood to be purely private and individualistic. Public affairs and social problems were thought to be beyond the sphere of spirituality. And finally the spirituality we inherit tends to rely upon God to intervene in his own good time to put right what is wrong with the world. That leaves very little for human beings to do except to pray for God's intervention.

It hardly needs saying that this kind of faith and this type of spirituality has no biblical foundation. The Bible does not separate the human person from the world in which he or she lives... A truly biblical spirituality would penetrate into every aspect of human existence and would exclude nothing from God's redemptive will. Biblical faith is prophetically relevant to everything that happens in the world.

The Kairos Document: Challenge to the Church.

ooooooooooo

The greatest religious problem today is how to be both a mystic and a militant; in other words, how to combine the search for an expansion of inner awareness with effective social action, and how to find one's true identity in both.

Ursula King: quoted by K Jones, Social Spirituality: Resurgence, Jan/Feb, 1989.

ooooooooooo

EARTHSONG

> If you can dream - and not make dreams your master;
> If you can think - and not make thoughts your aim,...
> Yours is the earth and everything that's in it.

Rudyard Kipling: If.

Karl Marx who was right about so many things - more right than nearly all the Christians of his time - was nevertheless wrong in assuming that all our ills, all human alienation (a better word than sin), springs from social and economic injustice. Only get social structures right and all will be well, and true harmony, true peace will be established. The dream is as false as the evangelical preacher's trust in individual conversion. Utopian politics are a recipe for disaster.

Paul Oestricher: The Double Cross.

Hurry is the curse of our century
and man, mopping the sweat from his forehead,
zigzags through life like a pawn in a fury
of being trapped on the board with his time expired.

Hurriedly we drink, hurriedly we love,
our souls eroding go to waste.
Hurriedly we push and shove
and later we repent, at haste.

But at least once, whether your home
in the world is sleeping or boiling with untruths,
stop, like a horse smothered in foam
sensing the abyss before its hooves.

For God's sake stop, even half way,
trust Heaven, as you would your fate,
think - even if you do not pray
to God - at least of your own state.

When the collapsing leaves flutter,
when the locomotive gives its hoarse cry,
know this: the tired runner is pitiful,
the one who has stopped stands high.

Sweep off the dust of vanity of vanities,
at last remember eternity,
and holy indecision will freeze
your feet to immobility.

There is strength in indecision
when you hesitate to follow
the path leading to perdition
at the end of which false beacons glow.

As you trample on people's faces like leaves,
stop! Like Vij*, you are blind.
Don't forego this last reprieve
by rushing on with a mad wind.

When you stride so confidently towards your goal
over bodies as though they were steps,
stop - have you forgotten God -
you are really stepping on yourself!

When spite is shoving you forward,
making your own soul a hypocrite,
towards the disgrace of a shot or a word -
don't hurry, don't do it!

Stop, O people of the Earth as you run
so blindly to the next assault!
Bullet, freeze as you fly from the gun,
and you, bomb in mid-air, halt!

O man, whose very name is sacred,
lifting the prayer of your eyes like a periscope
over disintegration and hatred,
For God's sake stop, for God's sake stop!

*Vij is a blind monster-gnome of Ukranian folk-lore whose eyelids touch the ground; if his eyes are open nothing can be hidden from them.

Yevgeny Yevtushenko: Hurry is the Curse of Our Century.
translated by Geoffrey Dutton and Igor Mazhakoff Koriakin.

ccccccccccc

Nature's instructions are always slow, those of men are generally premature.

Emile Rousseau, 1762.

ccccccccccc

"The English are very slow. The Greeks are fast..They decide!"
"But each one decides differently."
"That is individualism."
"But it leads to chaos."
"We like chaos!"

Lawrence Durrell: Reflections on a Marine Venus.

ccccccccccc

Nature, to be commanded, must be obeyed.

Francis Bacon: Novum Organum, 1620.

ccccccccccc

EARTHSONG

To every thing, turn - turn - turn,
There is a season, turn - turn - turn,
And a time to every purpose under heaven.

A time to be born
A time to die

A time to plant
A time to reap

A time to kill
A time to heal

A time to laugh
A time to weep

To every thing, turn - turn - turn,
There is a season, turn - turn - turn,
And a time to every purpose under heaven.

A time to build up
A time to break down

A time to dance
A time to mourn

A time to cast away stones
A time to gather stones together

To every thing, turn - turn - turn,
There is a season, turn - turn - turn,
And a time to every purpose under heaven.

A time of love
A time of hate

A time of war
A time of peace

A time you may embrace
A time to refrain from embracing

To every thing, turn - turn - turn,
There is a season, turn - turn - turn,
And a time to every purpose under heaven.

A time to gain
A time to loose

A time to rend
A time to sow

A time of love
A time of hate

A time of peace
I swear it's not too late.

To every thing, turn - turn - turn,
There is a season, turn - turn - turn,
And a time to every purpose under heaven.

To every thing, turn - turn - turn,
There is a season, turn - turn - turn,
And a time to every purpose under heaven.

Pete Seeger: Turn - Turn - Turn.

God said 'let there be light and dark and sun and moon and stars and dry land and hills and valleys and woods and streams and all manner of plants and insects and birds and animals and people; and let them fear and fight and feel pain but let them also feel desire and joy and love. Let the wind carry the sound of their suffering but let it carry the sound of their laughter too, let them grow old but let them give birth, let them toil but let them dance, let there be sorrow but let there be ecstasy; let them work on the world but let the world work on them; let what may happen, happen; but above all let them learn from their mistakes'.

Stephen Dunstone: God's First Draft.

Wisdom of serpent be thine,
Wisdom of raven be thine,
  Wisdom of valiant eagle.

Voice of swan be thine,
Voice of honey be thine,
  Voice of the son of the stars.

Bounty of sea be thine,
Bounty of land be thine,
  Bounty of the Father of heaven.

Esther de Waal: The Celtic Vision.

7
Tongues in Trees

And this our life,..
Finds tongues in trees, books in the running brooks,
Sermons in stones, and good in everything.

As You Like It, Act 2, scene 1.

But ask now the beasts and they shall teach thee;
and the fowls of the air, and they shall tell thee:
or speak to the earth, and it shall teach thee;
and the fishes of the sea shall declare unto thee.

Job: 12,7-8: Revised Version.

It is an important and popular fact that things are not always what they seem. For instance, on the planet Earth, man had always assumed that he was more intelligent than dolphins because he had achieved so much - the wheel, New York, wars and so on - whilst all the dolphins had ever done was muck about in the water having a good time. But conversly, the dolphins had always believed that they were far more intelligent than man - for precisely the same reasons.

Douglas Adams: The Hitch Hiker's Guide to the Galaxy.

For me, trees have always been the most penetrating preachers. I revere them when they live in tribes and families, in forests and groves. And even more I revere them when they stand alone. They are like lonely persons. Not like hermits who have stolen away out of some weakness, but like great solitary people, like Beethoven and Nietzsche. In their highest boughs the world rustles; their roots rest in infinity, but they do not lose themselves there; they struggle with all the force of their lives for one thing only: to fulfil themselves according to their own laws; to build up their own form; to represent themselves.

Hermann Hesse: Wandering.

EARTHSONG

Here then comes the consolation of the trees, the fragrance of shade, the blossoming of depth, shade that opens
and changes into light,
Light scented with shade, the intimacy of opening, the soul blossomed into its distance,
fed, found again, turned in again to itself, at the sources of the measureless, flush with the intimacy of shade,
inside the light-and-shade which is our deepest day.
Here begins the perpetual passing on, the crossing of moving frontiers,
like a sudden change of realm - without the appearences shifting,
Between two patches of sun a slope of cool pulls our face, a cool different from the night's spreading,
breath of a spring mixed with smell of pines,
a crude and balsam cool...
less than an exhalation the *idea* of cool, the print of another life,
and the air grows in the distance, fills with murmurs and with quiverings,
and the world's substance swells our breast, flows down the rivers of the blood,
bathes our furthest, finest roots,
at last we are inhabiting the murmur, our whole body is filled with a delicate and multitudinous speech...

O season of the long day, teach us towards evening the language of the forest, the passage among the tree-trunks who turn their faces away,
that long, insinuating phrase which does not want to teach anyone anything,
transmits patiently a secret entrusted,
a confidence on the scale of the universe, to the measure of the intimacy of the soul.
The consolation of the trees, towards evening.

Jean Mambrino: In the forests of Halin, 15th August 1978.
Translated by Jonathan Griffin.
Temenos: vol 1, pp 110-114

I think that I shall never see
A poem lovely as a tree
A tree whose hungry mouth is pressed
Against the earth's sweet flowing breast;
A tree that looks at God all day,
And lifts her leafy arms to pray;

A tree that may in summer wear
A nest of robins in her hair;
Upon whose bosom snow has lain;
Who intimately lives with rain.
Poems are made by fools like me,
But only God can make a tree.

Traditional Irish: quoted by Satish Kumar. A Sacred Journey. 'Resurgence', May-June 1988.

∞∞∞∞∞∞

O never harm the dreaming world,
the world of green, the world of leaves,
but let its million palms unfold
the adoration of the trees...

Kathleen Raine.

∞∞∞∞∞∞

Trees are the earth's endless effort to speak to the listening heaven.

Rabindranath Tagore: Fireflies.

∞∞∞∞∞∞

There were three little owls in a wood
Who sang hymns whenever they could;
What the words were about
One could never make out,
But one felt it was doing them good.

Unknown: Ring Out Wild Bells.

∞∞∞∞∞∞

In this brown husk a dale of hawthorn dreams,
A ceder in this narrow cell is thrust.
That will drink deeply of a century's streams.
These lilies shall make summer on my dust.

Here in their safe and simple house of death,
Sealed in their shells, a million roses leap.
Here I can blow a garden with my breath,
And in my hand a forest lies asleep.

Muriel Stuart: The Seed Shop.

∞∞∞∞∞∞

Each bush and oak doth know I AM

Henry Vaughan.

∞∞∞∞∞∞

EARTHSONG

That is rain on dry ground. We heard it:
We saw the little tempest in the grass,
The panic of anticipation: heard
The uneasy leaves flutter, the air pass
In a wave, the fluster of the vegetation;
Heard the first spatter of drops, the outriders
Larruping on the road, hitting against
The gate of the drought, and shattering
On to the lances of the tottering meadow.
It is rain; it is rain on dry ground,

Rain riding suddenly out of the air,
Battering the bare walls of the sun.
It is falling on to the tongue of the blackbird,
Into the heart of the thrush; the dazed valley
Sings it down. Rain, rain on dry ground!...
The rain stops.
The air is sprung with green.
The intercepted drops
Fall at their leisure; and between
The threading runnels on the slopes
The snail drags his caution into the sun.

Christopher Fry: The Boy With A Cart.

I come in little things,
Saith the Lord:
Not borne on morning wings
Of Majesty, but I have set my Feet
Amidst the delicate and bladed wheat
That springs triumphant in the furrowed sod.
There I do dwell, in weakness and in power:
Not broken or divided, saith our God!
In your strait garden plot I come to flower:
About your porch My Vine
Meek, fruitful, doth entwine:
Waits, at the threshold, love's appointed hour.

I come in little things,
Saith the Lord:
Yea! on glancing wings
Of eager birds, the softly pattering feet
Of furred and gentle beasts, I come to meet
Your hard and wayward heart. In brown bright eyes
That peep from out the brake, I stand confest
On every nest,
Where feathery patience is content to brood
And leaves her pleasure for the high emprize
Of motherhood -
There doth My Godhead brood.

Evelyn Underhill

It ain't a picture show. It ain't something you can look at apart from everything else, including yourself. I believe God is everything. Everything that is or ever was or ever will be. And when you can feel that, and be happy to feel that you've found it... My first step away from the old white man was trees. Then air. Then birds. Then other people. But one day when I was sitting quiet and feeling like a motherless child, which I was, it come to me: that feeling of being part of everything, not separate at all. I knew that if I cut a tree my arm would bleed. And I laughed and I cried and I run all round the house. I knew just what it was. In fact when it happen you can't miss it.'

Alice Walker: The Color Purple.

We have dreamed dreams beyond our comprehending,
    Visions too beautiful to be untrue,
    We have seen mysteries that yield no clue;
And sought our goals on ways that have no ending.
We creatures of the earth,
The lowly born, the mortal, the foredoomed
To spend our fleeting moments on the spot
Wherein tomorrow we shall be entombed
And hideously rot -
We have seen the loveliness that shall not pass,
We have beheld immortal destinies;
We have seen Heaven and Hell and joined their strife;
Ay, we whose flesh shall perish as the grass
Have flung the passion of the heart that dies
Into the hope of everlasting life.

Sidney Royse Lysaght.

There were no famous temples in Kalakankar, no historical monuments, no rare sights in this lonely land, with its scorched earth and dirty villages. The colours were not bright, the peasents wore nothing but plain white, the dusty foliage of the trees was dull. There was nothing exotic about the place, none of the fairytale quality that tourists sought in India. But instead, present in everything, permeating everything, there was an impossible deep sound, like that of an organ. If you remained very quiet, if you sat still gazing at the river, you too would hear it. You would sense it coming as a slow, reverberating gong, as the quietly breathing heart of a mighty, eternal life, in which everything - the earth, the river, the sky, the birds, and man - found itself blended. Even he who knows not God, who does not believe in Him, would, without knowing it, thank Him for the peace that filled his soul, and involuntarily, as though against his will, the words would escape him: Lord what bliss!

Svetlana Alliluyeva: Only One Year.

ꝏꝏꝏꝏꝏꝏ

In Churches and Cathedrals
I sought for God in vain:
He does not live imprisoned,
Or bound by priestly chain.
I asked of Mother Nature
If she could give the clue,
She bade me seek the silence
To find the answer true.

M. A. St Clair Stobart: Spiritual Songs for Congregational Singing.

ꝏꝏꝏꝏꝏꝏ

There's a body out there. A specimen.
The earth is shouting.
She was my mother.
Quick, muzzle her, muffle her up
Before anyone sees.
(A little more
carbon burned
a few less trees.)
If this gets rustled
we
will never
(love ever?)
be able
to get it all
back again.
In the beginning
This was
she
was
everything.

Sue Lightfoot: Gaia.

ꝏꝏꝏꝏꝏꝏ

One day, in a small village in Bengal, an ascetic woman from the neighbourhood came to see me. She had the name "Sarvakhepi" given to her by the village people, the meaning of which is "the woman who is mad about all things". She fixed her star-like eyes upon my face and startled me with the question, "When are you coming to meet me underneath the trees?" Evidently she pitied me who lived (according to her) prisoned behind walls, banished away from the great meeting-place of the All, where she had her dwelling. Just at that moment my gardener came with his basket, and when the woman understood that the flowers in the vase on my table were going to be thrown away, to make place for the fresh ones, she looked pained and said to me, "You are always engaged reading and writing; you do not see." Then she took the discarded flowers in her palms, kissed them and touched them with her forehead, and reverently murmured to herself, "Beloved of my heart." I felt that this woman, in her direct vision of the infinite personality in the heart of all things, truly represented the spirit of India.

Rabindranath Tagore.

To see a World in a grain of sand
And a Heaven in a Wild Flower,
Hold Infinity in the palm of your hand
And Eternity in an hour.

William Blake: Auguries of Innocence.

A snake came to my water-trough
On a hot, hot day, and I in pyjamas for the heat;
To drink there.

In the deep, strange-scented shade of the great dark carob-tree
I came down the steps with my pitcher
And must wait, must stand and wait, for there he was at the trough before me.

He reached down from a fissure in the earth-wall in the gloom
And trailed his yellow-brown slackness soft-bellied down, over the edge of the stone trough
And rested his head upon the stone bottom,
And where the water had dripped from the tap, in a small clearness,
He sipped with his straight mouth,
Softly drank through his straight gums, into his slack long body,
Silently

Someone was before me at my water-trough,
And I, like a second comer, waiting.

He lifted his head from his drinking, as cattle do,
And looked at me vaguely, as drinking cattle do,
And flickered his two-forked tongue from his lips, and mused a moment,
And stopped and drank a little more,
Being earth-brown, earth-golden from the burning bowels of the earth

EARTHSONG

On the day of Sicilian July, with Etna smoking.

The voice of my education said to me
He must be killed,
For in Sicily the black, black snakes are innocent, the gold are venomous.

And voices in me said, If you were a man
You would take a stick and break him now, and finish him off.

But must I confess how I liked him,
How glad I was he had come like a guest in quiet, to drink at my water-trough.
And depart peaceful, pacified, and thankless,
Into the burning bowels of this earth?

Was it cowardice, that I dared not kill him?
Was it perversity, that I longed to talk to him?
Was it humility, to feel so honoured?
I felt so honoured.

And yet those voices:
If you were not afraid, you would kill him!

And truly I was afraid, I was most afraid,
But even so honoured still more
That he should seek my hospitality
From out the dark door of the secret earth.

He drank enough
And lifted his head, dreamily, as one who has drunken,
And flickered his tongue like a forked night on the air; so black;
Seeming to lick his lips,
And looked around like a god, unseeing, into the air,
And slowly turned his head,
And slowly, very slowly, as if thrice adream,
Proceeded to draw his slow length curving round
And climb again the broken bank of my wall-face.

And as he put his head into that dreadful hole,
And as he slowly drew up, snake-easing his shoulders, and entered farther,
A sort of horror, a sort of protest against his withdrawing into that horrid black hole,
Deliberately going into the blackness, and slowly drawing himself after,
Overcame me now his back was turned.

I looked round, I put down my pitcher,
I picked up a clumsy log
And I threw it at the water-trough with a clatter.

I think it did not hit him,
But suddenly that part of him that was left behind convulsed in undignified haste,
Writhed like lightening, and was gone
Into the black hole, the earth-lipped fissure in the wall front,
At which, in the intense still noon, I stared with fascination.

And immediately I regretted it.
I thought how paltry, how vulgar, what a mean act!
I despised myself and the voices of my accursed human education.

And I thought of the albatross,
And I wished he would come back, my snake.

For he seemed to me again like a king,
Like a king in exile, uncrowned in the underworld,
Now due to be crowned again.

And so, I missed my chance with one of the lords
Of life.
And I have something to expiate;
A pettiness.

D H Lawrence: Snake.

Lord, help us to hear
The rock, the fish,
The beast, the bird,
The multitudinous
Elements
And be
Tender as the opening leaf
That answers to Your call.

Euanie Tippett.

I am a child born of fire
for all the earth's beginnings
sing in me.

I am a child out of time
born of pain
for all the earth's deaths
end with me.

I am a child born of love
out of light,
for you meet me here.

I am a child full of joy
born to live
and all the earth's surprises
dance in me.

I am a child born of spirit
wholeness unfolding
adorable silence
and all the earth's journeys
well up in me.

Erna Colebrook: Earth Song.

EARTHSONG

Deep within us all there is an amazing inner sanctuary of the soul, a holy place, a Divine Centre, a speaking Voice, to which we may continuously return. Eternity is at our hearts, pressing upon our time-torn lives, warming us with intimations of an astounding destiny, calling us home unto Itself. Yielding to those persuasions, gladly committing ourselves in body and soul, utterly and completely, to the Light Within, is the beginning of true life. It is a dynamic centre, a creative Life that presses to birth within us. It is a Light Within which illumines the face of God and casts shadows and new glories on the face of man. It is a seed stirring to life if we do not choke it. Here is the slumbering Christ, stirring to be awakened, to become the soul we clothe in earthly form and action. And He is within us all.

Thomas Kelly: A Testament of Devotion.

Wise woman of earth, I bring my question.
    Ask.
What is the sacred name of God?

    Men say it is too sacred
    to be pronounced.

In sorrow we perform our rituals of prayer,
and He does not answer.
He must be named.

    Long ago, when God walked on earth
    men hid his true name for safekeeping.
    So diligent were they, the sacred hiding-place
    itself was lost
    the secret forgotten.

I know you know it.
Could the name be Love?

    My dear, have you forgotten that too?
    Love is the sacred name for Human, man and woman.

Is it Radiance then?
Light inseparable from darkness?

    No, Radiance is the sacred name for spirit
    which contains light of sun and infinite
    dark between stars.

Infinite! That surely is the secret name
the unimaginable, the immense mystery!

    No. That is the sacred name for Within.

Is it Nothingness?

It is not. That is the lie of Reality.

Truth?

Truth is what it says.
Truth is the name for itself.

God. The secret name. The sacred name.
Is it That-Which-Can-Never-Be-Known?

Dear one, that is the sacred name for Thou.

Is it Life?

Oh no. Life is the true name for Earth.

Is it death?

The sacred name for Womb.

Where shall I find it, the name for God,
the true name? I must have it.
If I could speak it
I would have God at my grace-
as magicians,
knowing the names of rabbits and winds
can call them up and make them obey.
If I could speak the sacred name of God
He would be at my command
and I could summon Him
to do my work.

God! God!

Hush. No one answers that call.
You were born with the name on your lips.
Listen. I'll give it to you again, lightly
as the sound of an owl in the roar of loneliness
and you'll know it as true
as layers of pain flake off you like dead skin
(only those who die can know it a second time)

and when you hear it, listen deep in your body.
It is not for praising, not for worshipping
not for celebrating in idols outside yourself
or guarding as a secret.

It's for speaking simply, clearly, with joy
every day, every minute:

I am! I am!
The sacred name of God.

Jeni Couzyn: The Name of God.

8

A Time to Build

In the vacant places
We will build with new bricks
There are hands and machines
And clay for new brick
And lime for new mortar
Where the bricks are fallen
We will build with new stone
Where the beams are rotten
We will build with new timbers
Where the word is unspoken
We will build with new speech
There is work together...
And a job for each.

T. S. Eliot, Chorus from 'The Rock'.

I call heaven and earth to witness against you this day, that I have set before you life and death, the blessing and the curse: therefore choose life.

Deuteronomy: 30, 19. Revised Version.

Martin Luther was once asked what he would do if he knew that the world would end the next day. He replied, 'I would plant an apple tree'.

Were the world to end tomorrow
would we plant a tree today?
Would we till the soil of loving,
Kneel to work and rise to pray?

Dare we try to give an answer,
reaching out with fragile hope;
touching lives with words of Easter,
break a loaf and share a cup?

Pray that at the end of living,
of philosophies and creeds,
God will find his people busy
planting trees and saving seeds.

Fred Kaan: Planting Trees and Sowing Seeds.

EARTHSONG

At the Sixth Assembly of the World Council of Churches in 1983, meeting in Vancouver, Canada, delegates of churches from all over the world asked the WCC to engage churches "in a conciliar process of mutual commitment to justice, peace and the integrity of creation".

The delegates spoke out of their own situations and experience. Some came from situations of intense human suffering. Where many have little or nothing and a few have more than enough. Where human rights are violated. Where people face discrimination and are treated as less than human because of the colour of their skin, ethnic origin or sex. They spoke of justice not simply as a concept, but as a cry for vindication. That what is wrong be set right.

Some came from war-torn countries where military conflict is formented and maintained by selfish interest groups. Still others came from situations where nuclear weapons are in place as grim reminders of an impending holocaust. For them, too, peace was not just an idea. It was a yearning for a new world order in which wars and threats of wars will cease.

Others were conscious of the terrible violence done to creation - to nature and human beings - in the insatiable drive for human progress. Polluted air and water, diminishing natural resources, continuing extinction of forms of plant and animal life. Here, too, the integrity of creation was not viewed as a mere concept. It was a plea to recognise that we live in an interdependent world - a world of relationships and delicate balances.

They listened to each other. They realised that the struggles for justice, for peace and for the integrity of creation were interlinked. They had to be one cohesive struggle for life. To confront the powers of death with power of Jesus Christ - the Life of the World.

World Council of Churches: Justice, Peace and the Integrity of Creation.

ooooooooooo

This is no ordinary battle. There are no weapons involved; no military commanders; no opposing nation or religious divides. And the only enemy is *ourselves.* The Battle for the Planet is a battle for our own survival.

Jonathon Porritt: in André Singer: Battle for the Planet.

ooooooooooo

It is a war in which all nations must be allies... No attempt to protect the environment will be successful in the long run unless ordinary people - the Californian housewife, the Mexican peasent, the Soviet factory worker, the Chinese farmer - are willing to adjust their life-styles. Our wasteful, careless ways must become a thing of the past. We must .. do a thousand things differently in our everyday lives. We owe this not only to ourselves but also to the unborn generations who will one day inherit the earth...

Let there be no illusions. Taking effective action to halt the massive injury to the earth's environment will require a mobilization of political will, international cooperation and sacrifice unknown except in wartime.

Thomas Sancton: Time International, January 1989.

To live we must daily break the body and shed the blood of creation. When we do this knowingly, lovingly, skillfully and reverently it is a sacrament. When we do it ignorantly, greedily, clumsily and destructively it is a desecration. In such desecration we condemn ourselves to spiritual and moral loneliness and others to want.

Wendell Berry: The Gift of Good Land.

Teach your children
what we have taught our children,
that the earth is our mother.
Whatever befalls the earth
befalls the sons of earth.
If men spit upon the ground,
they spit upon themselves.

This we know.
The earth does not belong to man;
man belongs to earth.
This we know.
All things are connected
like the blood
which unites one family.

All things are connected.
Whatever befalls the earth
befalls the sons of earth.
Man did not weave the web of life,
he is merely a strand in it.
Whatever he does to the web,
he does to himself.

Chief Seattle.

'Tell me the weight of a snowflake,' a coalmouse asked a wild dove.

'Nothing more than nothing', was the answer.

'In that case, I must tell you a marvellous story', the coalmouse said. 'I sat on the branch of a fir close to its trunk, not in a raging blizzard: no, just in a dream, without a sound and without any violence. Since I did not have anything better to do, I counted the snowflakes settling on the twigs and needles of my branch. Their number was exactly 3,741,952. When the 3,741,953rd dropped onto the branch - nothing more than nothing, as you say - the branch broke off'.

Having said that, the coalmouse flew away.

The dove, since Noah's time an authority on the matter, thought about the story for a while and finally said to herself: 'Perhaps there is only one person's voice lacking for peace to come to the world.'

Kurt Kauter: New Fables, Thus spoke the Marabou.

The Japanese monkey *Macaca fuscata* has been observed in the wild for a period of over 30 years.

In 1952 on the island of Koshima scientists were providing monkeys with sweet potatoes dropped on the sand. The monkeys liked the raw sweet potatoes, but they found the dirt unpleasent. An 18-month-old female named Imo found she could solve the problem by washing the potatoes in a nearby stream. She taught this trick to her mother. Her playmates also learned this new way and they taught their mothers, too.

This cultural innovation was gradually picked up by various monkeys. Between 1952 and 1958, all the young monkeys learned to wash the sandy sweet potatoes to make them more palatable. Only the adults who imitated their children learned this social improvement. Other adults kept eating the dirty sweet potatoes.

Then something startling took place, In the autumn of 1958, a certain number of Koshima monkeys were washing sweet potates - the exact number is not known. Let us suppose that when the sun rose there were 99. Let's further suppose that later that morning the hundredth monkey learned to wash potatoes. THEN IT HAPPENED! By that evening almost all the monkeys were washing sweet potatoes before eating them.

Ken Keyes: The Hundredth Monkey.

In our hands now lies not only our own future, but that of all other living creatures with whom we share the earth.

David Attenborough: Life on Earth.

Lord, may we love all your creation, all the earth and every grain of sand in it. May we love every leaf, every ray of light. May we love the animals: you have given them the rudiments of thought and joy untroubled. Let us not trouble them; let us not harass them, let us not deprive them of their happiness, let us not work against your intent.

For we acknowledge unto you that all is like an ocean, all is flowing and blending, and that to withhold any measure of love from anything in your universe is to withhold that same measure from you.

Feodor Dostoevsky, The Brothers Karamazov.

May the peace of Christ prevail - may life be so expensive, no person will deprive another of it. May bread be so cheap that no child on earth will go to bed hungry. May our skies be always blue; the grass ever green; our children have sweets in their mouths and a glass of milk every day. May the peace of Christ prevail.

Christie Rosa, Asian Christian Peace Conference.

Christ has no body now on earth but ours,
no hands but ours
no feet but ours.
Ours are the eyes through which is to look at Christ's compassion on the world.
Ours are the feet with which he is to go about doing good.
Ours are hands with which he is to bless men and women now.

St Teresa of Avila.

You are never given a wish
without also being given
the power to make it come true.
You may have to work for it, however.

There is no such thing as a problem
without a gift for you in its hands.
You seek problems
because you need their gifts.

Messiah's Handbook: Reminders for the Advanced Soul.

The Rainbow Covenant

Brothers and sisters in creation, we covenant this day with you and with all creation yet to be;

> With every living creature and all that contains and sustains you.
>
> With all that is on earth and with the earth itself;
>
> With all that lives in the waters and with the waters themselves;
>
> With all that flies in the skies and with the sky itself.

We establish this covenant, that all our powers will be used to prevent your destruction.

We confess that it is our kind who put you at risk of death.

We ask for your trust and as a symbol of our intention we mark our covenant with you by the rainbow.

This is the sign of the covenant between ourselves and every living thing that is found on the earth.

World Wildlife Fund: Winchester harvest celebration, 1987.

And the rainbow stood on the earth that new clean naked bodies would issue to a new generation, to a new growth; rising to the light and the wind and the clean rain of heaven.

D H Lawrence: The Rainbow.

Epilogue

A GENTLER EARTH

Tread softly because you tread on my dreams.

W. B. Yeats.

Many of the oldest British literary texts belong to our Welsh heritage. They tell tales of bravery, the stories of saints and the legends of King Arthur whose famous deeds were sung all over Europe and who it was believed would come back one day to save his people.

They also tell us that the Welsh people revered the salmon, who was for our ancestors a symbol of wisdom. This fish spends all its adult life in the wideness of the salty oceans and swims up the great rivers to spawn and give birth to a new generation in the sweetness of small turbulent streams in the hills and mountains from where it originally came. It is a fish which over the aeons of time has explored and made all the waters of the earth its home and is comfortable and at ease there. It is a creature in perfect harmony with its surroundings.

What a panoply of diversity creation has brought forth! What a delight. What a feast for our eyes. No wonder nature programmes are winners on television.

We, the human species, are also part of this diversity and creativity. The creative process, is also at work in us: it is our basic need and driving force. It is a gift which every living person on this planet posseses. With this creative spirit we have built the marvellous world we see around us. From it spring all our relationships with the earth and with one another.

What do we see?

Villages in fertile valleys and arid deserts, great big concrete cities on all the continents, cultures, lifestyles, races, languages, religions, medicin, art, all manner of educational facilities, the sciences, agricultural practices, political and economic systems, industrial complexes to create consumer goods for our basic needs and comforts, defence ideologies, communication systems, sport and recreational facilities, and, to keep it all in order, law and government.

Above all we see people. People enthusiastically building and creating. Thinking, relating, loving, reproducing, knowing, having imagination, being inspired, transforming, integrating, organising, inventing, designing, building, meditating and asking questions. Earths incredible creative spirit mushrooms and unfolds ever outwards and in the doing we all have to live in an ever more complicated sort of place.

EARTHSONG

When we consider that the human population has doubled in only one generation from 2.5 billion to over 5 billion, we begin to grasp the enormity of our undertaking and we marvel that things have gone so well! Life is extraordinarily resiliant and adaptable. Yet in every face we meet in the street or on television, we read a hidden anxiety and our compassion flows out to each and every one. Our creative enthusiasm is overwhelming us, strangling us, poisoning us. We are busy poisoning the hand and heart that feeds us.

The whole world is alive with plants and animals, with people, with their ideas and beliefs and with all the things they have made. A world full of diversity, full of tension, a world in germination. Each human being with an identity, with roots, with things he or she is good at creating. "Where do you come from?" and "What do you do?" are so often our first questions on meeting a stranger. Each one a person of selfworth and dignity, with an inner strength, an outer smile and a sense of belonging to this earth. Each person precious and unique. Each one with a will and purpose.

But, at times our creative spirit runs away with us, we become over-enthusiastic, wilful, manipulative, self-centred and hateful. We start loosing our way, making creativity our master. The structures we build up cause our enslavement. This creativity, which no longer helps and serves us, is no longer a blessing, is no longer for the good of all. We no longer feel free - we do not see a future for our children. We must reject these structures as having outlived their usefulness, as unable to stand the test of time. When we are able to see our own wilfulness, when our eyes are opened, we feel very vulnerable, defenceless, powerless, even naked: but free. Free to listen again to the true creative spirit within us - full of hope to begin to do things differently.

Our creative spirit is like a living stream, ever seeking and searching to flow out, to unfold in uncharted channels. To be able to go foward we now need to take a long look backwards: it is time for us to make a journey upstream, to travel back in time. To try to understand the workings of the creative spirit, not only in ourselves but in the world we live in and in the whole of the universe. With the help of scientists, philosophers, theologians, we are just beginning to unravel concepts of spontaneous creation of increasingly complex systems of order out of chaos by self-organisation in freedom within the constraints of law and necessity: difficult ideas which are still shadowy and lack detail. For us, it suffices to know that the creative spirit is reliable, that it can be trusted, for it has stood the test of the whole of time right back to the Big Bang, emanating from the Word itself.

When we come to a deeper understanding of the divisions and tensions in the world as a dynamic unfolding of its true wealth and beauty and perceive our common past as a mysterious whole with inner unity and vigour, a transformation can take place which liberates us to a new awareness. A new indwelling spirit of global interdependence comes to birth at the centre of our being. With heaven in our heart and gifts in our hands we shall bring hope and healing until the whole earth shines like a jewel in the universe. Paradoxically it means a commitment to begin all over again and find new and relevant ways of being enabling communities right where we live, in our block of flats, street or locality; not a backwater, but as much the centre of the universe as anywhere else, and part of the web of life. It will require an act of faith in ourselves and in the goodwill of others to embrace our immediate, often estranged, neighbours in our new emerging awareness.

If we honour our roots, revere and celebrate the earth's diversity, tend all our connections, walk with gentleness and openness, and seek harmony day by day, our children *will* inherit the earth.

∞∞∞∞∞∞∞∞

An Affirmation for Life Today

- We believe in the interdependence, selfworth and fulfilment of all life on earth.
- *We believe that like a mother, God is on the side of life.*

∞ ∞ ∞ ∞ ∞

- We believe that the earth contains all the resources to sustain a true sharing community of the human family through prudent global housekeeping, now and for all future generations.
- *We believe that like a mother God provides for all her children.*

∞ ∞ ∞ ∞ ∞

- We believe that every person is called, through participation and open partnership, to nurture and promote the vision of interdependence, selfworth and fulfilment of all creation.
- *We believe that like a mother, God takes delight in watching her children grow up.*

∞ ∞ ∞ ∞ ∞

- We believe in a dynamic, unfolding universe as the holy centre and embodiment of our creator God.
- *We believe that like a mother, God brings all creation to birth. She loves all, risks all, suffers all, sustains all and is all in all.*

∞ ∞ ∞ ∞ ∞

- We believe that God desires the wellbeing and wholeness of all creation and that Jesus Christ offers the human race healing and hope as cosmic lover, guide and liberator of life.
- *We believe that like a mother, God knows all, feels all, bears all, embraces all, transforms all and brings new life.*

Bibliography

PRINCIPAL SOURCES AND FURTHER READING

Ansell, J., Hunt, J., McFlynn, G. & Matthews, G. *Prayers for Peacemakers.* Kevin Mayhew, 1988.

Attenborough, David. *Life on Earth.* Collins, 1979.

Barnaby, Frank. (Ed) *The Gaia Peace Atlas.* Pan Books, 1988.

Basset, Elizabeth. *Love is My Meaning.* Darton, Longman & Todd, 1986.

Berry, Wendell. *The Gift of Good Land.* North Point Press, San Francisco, 1981.

Bonhoeffer, D. *Letters and Papers from Prison.* Fontana Books, 1959.

Brandt Commission. *Common Crisis. North-South: Cooperation for World Recovery.* Pan Books, 1983.

Cadbury's. *Sixth Book of Children's Poetry.* Beaver Books, 1988.

Cassidy, Sheila. *Sharing the Darkness.* Darton, Longman and Todd, 1988.

de Chardin, Teilhard. *Hymn of the Universe.* Collins, 1965.

de Chardin, Teilhard. *The Phenomenon of Man.* Collins, 1983.

Couzyn, Jeni. *Life by Drowning, Selected Poems.* Bloodaxe Books, 1985.

Dauncey, Guy. *After the Crash. The Emergence of the Rainbow Economy.* Green Print, 1988

Davies, Paul. *God and the New Physics.* Pelican Books, 1984

Davies, Paul. *Superforce.* Unwin, 1985.

Davies, Paul. *Cosmic Blueprint.* Heinemann, 1987.

Dawkins, Richard. *The Blind Watchmaker.* Penguin Books, 1988.

Doyle, B. *Meditations with Julian of Norwich.* Bear & Co. 1983.

Durrell, Lawrence. *Reflections on a Marine Venus.* Faber, 1960.

Dylan, Bob. *Writings & Drawings.* Grafton Books, 1987.

Eliot, T S. *The Waste Land and other Poems.* Faber & Faber, 1940.

Findhorn Foundation. *Trees for Life Calendar, 1989*

Fox, Matthew. *Original Blessing.* Bear & Co. 1983.

Fox, Matthew. *The Coming of the Cosmic Christ.* Harper & Row, 1988

Fromm, Erich. *The Art of Loving.* Unwin, 1975.

Fromm, Erich. *To Have or To Be?* Abacus, 1979.

Fuller, Roy. *Fellow Mortals, an Anthology of Animal Verse.* Macdonald & Evans, 1981.

Gardner, Helen. *The New Oxford Book of English Verse.* OUP, 1972.

Garrison, J. *The Darkness of God: Theology after Hiroshima.* SCM Press, 1982.

George, Susan. *A Fate Worse Than Debt.* Penguin Books, 1988.

Gibran, Kahlil. *The Prophet.* Heinemann, 1980.

Giono, Jean. *The Man who Planted Trees.* Chelsea Green Publishing Company, 1987.

Gleick, James. *Chaos.* Heinemann, 1988.

Gollancz, Victor. *A Year of Grace.* Penguin Books, 1955.

Goudge, Elizabeth. *A Book of Comfort.* Collins, 1964.

Greene, Barbara and Victor Gollancz. *God of a Hundred Names.* Gollancz, 1972

Griffiths, Bede. *The Cosmic Revelation.* Collins, 1983.

Hamman, Henry and Stuart Parrott. *Mayday at Chernobyl.* New English Library, 1987.

Hartshorne, Charles. *The Divine Relativity: A Social Conception of God.* Yale University Press, 1948.

Humphrey, N. and Lifton, R.J. *In a Dark Time.* Faber & Faber, 1984.

Iona Community. *Service Book.* Wild Goose Publications, 1988

Jenkins, David. *God, Miracle and the Church of England.* SCM Press, 1987.

Jenkins, David. *God, Politics and the Future.* SCM Press, 1988

Jungk, Robert. *Brighter than a Thousand Suns.* Penguin Books, 1964.

The Kairos Document. *Challenge to the Church.* Catholic Institute for International Relations and the British Council of Churches. 1986.

Kelly, Thomas K. *A Testament of Devotion.* Quaker Home Service, 1979.

Keyes, Ken. *The Hundredth Monkey.* Vision Books, Oregon, 1985.

Kipling, Rudyard. *Just So Stories.* Macmillan, 1964

Lanzmann, Claude. *SHOAH.* Pantheon Books, New York, 1985.

Lovelock, J.E. *Gaia, a New Look at Life on Earth.* OUP, 1987.

McDonagh, Sean. *To Care for the Earth.* Geoffrey Chapman, 1986.

McFague, Sallie. *Models of God.* SCM Press, 1987.

McLuhan T. C. (Ed.) *Touch the Earth.* Abacus 1986.

Meadows, D. H., Meadows, D. L., Randep, J., Behrens, W. W. *The Limits to Growth. A Report for the Club of Rome's Project on the Predicament of Mankind.* Pan Books, 1974.

Moltmann, Jürgen. *The Trinity and the Kingdom of God.* SCM, 1981.

Moltmann, Jürgen. *God in Creation.* SCM Press, 1985

Myers. Norman. (Ed.) *The Gaia Atlas of Planet Management.* Pan Books, 1985.

Oestricher, Paul. *The Double Cross.* Darton, Longman and Todd, 1986.

Oppenheimer, Helen. *Looking Before and After.* Collins, 1988.

Palmer, Martin. (Ed.) *Creation Festival Liturgy, Coventry Cathredral.* WWF, 1988.

Palmer, Martin. *Genesis or Nemesis, belief, meaning and ecology.* Dryad Press, 1988.

Palmer, Martin and Anne Nash. (Ed.) *Advent and Ecology, Resources for Worship, Reflection and Action.* WWF, 1988.

Palmer, Martin, Anne Nash and Ivan Hattingh. (Ed) *Faith and Nature.* Rider, 1987.

Polkinghorne, John. *One World.* SPCK, 1986.

Polkinghorne, John. *Science and Creation.* SPCK, 1988

Polkinghorne, John. *Science and Providence.* SPCK, 1989

Prigogine, Ilya and Isabelle Stengers. *Order out of Chaos.* Flamingo, 1985.

Peacocke, Arthur. *God and the New Biology.* J M Dent, 1986

Raine, Kathleen. *Selected Poems.* Golgonooza Press, 1988.

Ramsay, Jay (Ed.) *Transformation: The Poetry of Spiritual Consciousness.* Rivelin Grapheme Press, 1988.

Reardon, John P. (Ed.) *Leaves from the Tree of Peace.* United Reformed Church.

Report of the Independent Commission on International Development Issues. *North-South: a Programme for Survival.* Pan Books, 1980. (The Brandt Report).

Report for the Independent Commission on International Humanitarian Issues. *Famine: A Man-made Disaster?* Pan Books, 1985

Runcie, Robert and Basil Hume. *Prayers for Peace.* SPCK, 1987

Robinson, John. *Exploration into God.* SCM Press, 1967.

Scheer, Robert. *With Enough Shovels.* Secker & Warburg, 1983.

Schell, Jonathan. *The Fate of the Earth.* Picador, 1982.

Schumacher, E.F. *Small is Beautiful.* Abacus, 1974.

Singer, A. *Battle for the Planet.* Pan Books, 1987.

Spretnak, Charlene. *The Spiritual Dimension of Green Politics.* Bear & Co. 1986.

Tagore, Rabindranath. *Gitanjali.* MacMillan.

Tillich, Paul. *The Shaking of the Foundations.* Penguin Books, 1962.

Thompson, William Irwin. *GAIA, A Way of Knowing.* Lindisfarne Press, 1987

Tripp, Rhoda Thomas. *The International Thesaurus of Quotations.* Penguin Books, 1979.

Uhlein, Gabrielle. *Meditations with Hildegarde of Bingen.* Bear & Co. 1983.

Vanstone, W H. *Love's Endeavour, Love's Expense.* Darton, Longman & Todd, 1977

Waal, Esther de. *The Celtic Vision.* Darton, Longman & Todd, 1988.

Walker, Alice. *The Color Purple.* The Women's Press, 1983

Weber, Renee. *Dialogues with Scientists and Sages.* Routledge & Kegan Paul, 1986.

Weizsäcker, Carl Friedrich von. *Die Zeit drängt. Eine Weltversammlung der Christen für Gerechtigkeit, Frieden und die Bewahrung der Schöpfung.* Carl Hanser Verlag, München, 1986.

Wood, Barbara. *One World God's World.* Bible Reading Fellowship, 1986.

Woodward, Zenka and Ian. *Ring Out Wild Bells.* Hutchinson, 1987.

World Commission on Environment and Development. *Our Common Future.* OUP, 1987. (The Brundtland Report)

World Council of Churches. *Justice, Peace and the Integrity of Creation.* WCC, 1987

World Wildlife Fund. *Creation and Harvest.* WWF, 1987.

Zukav, Gary. *The Dancing Wu Li Masters.* Flamingo, 1982.

Other Sources

Shruti Pankaj (p. 9) in Jay Ramsay (Ed). *Transformations.*
Rabindranath Tagore (p. 14). *Poems from Balaka.* John Murray, 1962.
Hildegarde of Bingen (pp. 15, 24, 25) in Gabrielle Uhlein. *Meditations with Hildegarde of Bingen.*
D. H. Lawrence (pp. 17, 93) in Vivian de Silva and Warren Roberts (Ed). *D. H. Lawrence, The Complete Poems.* Heinemann.
Isaac Newton (p. 17) *Optics, London, 1730*
Henri Atlan (p. 19) in William Irwin Thompson (Ed). *Gaia: A Way of Knowing.*
Ilya Prigogine (p. 21) in Renée Weber. *Dialogues with Scientists and Sages.*
Annie Dillard (p. 21). *Pilgrim at Tinker Creek.* Bantam Books, 1975.
Moyra Caldecott (p. 22) in Martin Palmer (Ed). *Creation Festival Liturgy.*
Mala Mason (p. 23) Yoga Today.
Evelyn Nolt (p. 25) in Belle Valerie Gaunt and George Trevelyan. *A Tent in Which to Pass a Summer Night.* Coventure, 1977.
Julian of Norwich (p. 28) in Brendon Doyle. *Meditations with Julian of Norwich.*
Pierre Teilhard de Chardin (p. 25). *Le Milieu Divin.*
D. H. Lawrence (p. 31). *A Selection from Phoenix.* Penguin Books, 1971.
Elsa Tamez (p. 31) in World Council of Churches. *New Eyes for Reading.* Quoted in 'Encounters', 1988, United Reformed Church.
Heather Harrison (p. 38) Birmingham Readers and Writers Festival, 1988. Quoted in 'Sanity', January 1989.
Richard Jeffries (p. 38) quoted in Barbara Greene and Victor Gollancz. *God of a Hundred Names.*
Helen Colebrook (pp. 39, 57) unpublished manuscripts.
James Joyce (p. 40) *Ulysses.* Penguin Books, 1983
St Francis of Assisi (p. 40) quoted in Sean McDonagh. *To Care for the Earth.*
Declaration of the Penan people, Borneo. (p. 43) quoted in Findhorn Foundation. *Trees for Life Calendar, 1989.*
The Jataka (p. 44) Pali Text Society, distributed by Routledge & Kegan Paul.
Siobhan Aiton (p. 44), **Danny Conners** (p. 45), **Sarah Butcher** (p. 45) in *Cadbury's Sixth Book of Children's Verse.*
Anne Stevenson (p. 45) *Selected Poems 1956-1986.* OUP.

S. Piper (p. 46) Unpublished manuscript.
Erna Colebrook (pp. 47, 93) unpublished manuscripts.
Sister Rosita Shiosee (p. 48) in World Council of Churches, JPIC Resource Pack 4. 6.
US Atom Test Observer, Christmas Island (p. 49) quoted in Robert Scheer. *With Enough Shovels.*
Roul Hilberg (p. 50) in Claude Lanzman. *SHOAH.*
W. B. Yeats (p. 51) in Helen Gardner. *The new Oxford Book of English Verse.*
Jean Anouilh (p. 54) *The Lark.* Methuen, 1955
F. C. Happold (p. 55) in Elizabeth Basset. *Love is my Meaning.*
Joseph Mary Plunkett (p. 56) in H Ward McGraw. *Prose and Poetry of England.* The Singer Company, 1934. Quoted in Sean McDonach. *To Care for the Earth.*
Chris Foster (p. 59) Integrity Publications, 1980.
Christopher Fry (p. 59) *A Sleep of Prisoners.* OUP, 1951.
Rainer Maria Rilke (p. 59) in Victor Gollancz. *A Year of Grace.* Penguin Books, 1955
Theodore Roethke (p. 61) in N. Humphrey and R. J. Lifton. *In a Dark Time.*
Wendell Berry (p. 69) Harcourt Brace, 1975.
Henry Miller (p. 69) Hatchards.
Hermann Hesse (p. 71) Peter Owen, 1970.
John Seed (p. 72) quoted in Findhorn Foundation. *Trees for Life Calendar, 1989.*
Messiah's Handbook (p. 73, 101) Richard Bach. *Illusions.* Pan Books, 1978.
E. F. Schumacher (p. 73) Green Party Manifesto.
Ralph Waldo Trine (p. 73) G. Bell, 1899.
Sydney Carter (p. 74)
Kahlil Gibran (p. 77) William Heinemann, 1954.
Blaise Pascal (p. 77) in Rhoda Thomas Tripp. *The International Thesaurus of Quotations.*
Yoruba poem (p. 77) in 'Encounters', 1988, United Reformed Church.
Mahatma Gandhi (p. 79)
Yevgeny Yevtushenko (p. 81) W. H. Allen, 1972.
Emile Rousseau (p. 81), **Francis Bacon** (p. 81) in Rhoda Thomas Tripp. *The International Thesaurus of Quotations.*
Pete Seeger (p. 83) *the Bitter and the Sweet.* Columbia Broadcasting System Inc.
Stephen Dunstone (p. 83)
Douglas Adams (p. 85) *The Hitch Hiker's Guide to the Galaxy.* Pan Books, 1979.
Hermann Hesse (p. 85) quoted in Findhorn Foundation. *Trees for Life Calendar, 1989.*
Henry Vaughan (p. 87) in Barbara Greene and Victor Gollancz. *God of a Hundred Names.*
Muriel Stuart (p. 87) in Elizabeth Goudge. *A Book of Comfort.*
Christopher Fry (p. 88) *The Boy with a Cart.* Muller, 1945.
Evelyn Underhill (p. 88) in Elizabeth Basset. *Love is my Meaning.*
Sidney Royse Lysaght (p. 89). *Beyond the Farthest Horizon.* Macmillan.
Svetlana Alliluyeva (p. 90) in Elizabeth Basset. *Love is my Meaning.*
Sue Lightfoot (p. 90) unpublished manuscript.
Rabindranath Tagore (p. 91). *The Gardener.* Macmillan.
William Blake (p. 91) in Elizabeth Basset. *Love is my Meaning.*
Euanie Tippett (p. 93) quoted in Devon Christian Ecology Group leaflet.

Fred Kaan (p. 97) *Planting Trees and Sowing Seeds.* OUP, *(in press).*
Chief Seattle (p. 99) in John P. Reardon (Ed). *Leaves from the Tree of Peace.*
Kurt Kauter (p. 100) in John P. Reardon (Ed). *Leaves from the Tree of Peace.*
Feodor Dostoevsky (p. 101) in Barbara Greene and Victor Gollancz. *God of a Hundred Names.*
Christie Rosa (p. 101) personal communication.
St Teresa of Avila (p. 101) in Elizabeth Basset. *Love is my Meaning.*
D. H. Lawrence (p. 102) *The Rainbow.* Penguin Books, 1988.

Index